HARLEY-DAVIDSON
Softail

GREG FIELD

MOTORBOOKS

This edition first published in 2003 by
Motorbooks International, an imprint of
MBI Publishing Company, Galtier Plaza,
Suite 200, 380 Jackson Street, St. Paul, MN
55101-3885 USA

Motorbooks International titles are also
available at discounts in bulk quantity for
industrial or sales-promotional use. For details
write to Special Sales Manager at Motorbooks
International Wholesalers & Distributors,
Galtier Plaza, Suite 200, 380 Jackson Street,
St. Paul, MN 55101-3885 USA.

ISBN 0-7603-1063-7

On the front cover: Unlike more flamboyant
efforts, the Deuce was evidence that Harley
knew the power of controlled subtley in styling.
Photo by Jeff Hackett

On the frontispiece: After successfully
recapturing the look of the hardtail rear
end on the original Softail in 1984, Harley-
Davidson then recaptured the look of the
springer front end on the Softail Springer
of 1988.

On the title page: Harley styling gurus Willie
G. Davidson and Louie Netz designed the
1990 Fat Boy to be reminiscent of the B-29
Superfortress bombers of World War II.

On the back cover: Harley's heritage allowed
for a unique twist on model innovation—the
1986 Heritage Softail—something new made
from something old.

About the Author:
Greg Field has written a number of books on the
subject of motorcycles, including several volumes
dealing with Harley-Davidson, including the
critically acclaimed *Harley-Davidson Evolution*
(Motorbooks International, 2001) and *Original
Harley-Davidson Panhead.*

Edited by Darwin Holmstrom
Designed by LeAnn Kuhlmann

Printed in China

CONTENTS

ACKNOWLEDGMENTS

In researching this book, I was fortunate to receive help from many of the most important contributors to the Softail story. I relied heavily on their memories to tell that story. Foremost among them is Bill Davis, the visionary engineer who designed the Softail frame.

Many thanks to the following former Harley-Davidson employees who were kind enough to spend many hours with me on the phone: Vaughn Beals, Rit Booth, John Davidson, Tom Gelb, Hank Hubbard, Ray Miennert, Dick O'Brien, Bob Sroka, Mark Tuttle, Don Valentine, and David Webster.

A whole host of others helped, too. If I have forgotten anyone in the following list, I hope they will forgive the oversight.

Employees of several Washington State Harley-Davidson franchises were enormously helpful in helping me locate motorcycles and in sharing information. In no particular order, they are John Martin and Scott Moon (Eastside Harley-Davidson); Fred Smith, Dave Nelson, and Jeff Arnold (Skagit Harley-Davidson); Carmen and Russ Tom and Bill Chase (Downtown Harley-Davidson); and Casey Wing, Barry Mercer, and Mike Gosson (Eastside's Harley Shop).

For allowing me the opportunity to photograph their motorcycles, I'd like to thank the following owners: John Adams (1986 Softail Custom), Jay Bennett (2002 Standard), Steve Birtle (1995 Heritage Classic), Rick Erickson (1988 Springer), Fred Faupel (1990 Fat Boy), Scott A. Hill (1997 Bad Boy), Doug Kelly (1993 Nostalgia), John Kline (2002 Fat Boy), Mattie Love (2001 Fat Boy), Albert McCaleb (1984 Softail), Greg Ochs (1994 Heritage Special), Jerry Rasmussen (2001 Deuce), Jerry Sanden (1986 Heritage and 1991 Springer Softails), Fred Smith (1984 Softail), and Howard Zang (1999 Night Train).

For helping me find some of the key bikes, thanks to Brock and Debbie Radloff of Classic Iron Works in Redmond, Washington.

Special thanks also to Stephan Byarlay for lending some critical materials at a critical time, Tom Murphy for all his contacts, Buzz Buzzelli (*American Rider* magazine), Kip Woodring, and Rob Carlson of Kokesh Motorcycles (Spring Lake Park, Minnesota).

Thanks to the following for contributing in myriad ways: Kevin Cruff and Teri Majka; Patrick, Patricia, and Nadine Bennett; Rick Mahnke of Moto Guzzi Cycle (Brooklyn, Wisconsin); Gerry and Susan Olson; Chuck, Sandy, and Julie Cossè, Bill and Sandy Banfield, and Dave Cotton.

For long-term encouragement and support, to my parents, Larry and Laurie; my siblings, Scot, Shawn, Dawn, and Heather; my grandmother, Gladys Field; and my good friends Jerry Beach, Todd Blakely, Owen Herman, Martyn Jessup, Kevin Lentz, Tim Lien, Barry Mercer, Tom Samuelsen, John Scharf, and Joe Sova.

For putting me up and putting up with me while in Milwaukee: Annie and Heidi Golembiewski; Ray, Carol, Tracie, Becky, Vicky, Katie, and Nicole Karshna; Ed and Jean Kwiecinski; and Jeff, Jackie, Olivia, and Nicholas Ciardo.

For tolerating my "fluid" deadlines, to Darwin Holmstrom and the rest of the staff at MBI Publishing.

Finally, to Jeni, who put up with so much obsessive behavior and gave up so much to provide me with the time needed to finish the manuscript.

INTRODUCTION

"It's not a motorcycle, baby, it's a chopper."

—Bruce Willis, in the movie *Pulp Fiction*

A new breed of Harley rider sprang up in the 1960s, and without the Motor Company's consent these newcomers redefined the future of Harley-Davidson motorcycles. While the girly-men of the era styled their hair and acted cool, these boys stylized their bikes and *were* cool. But even they weren't as cool as their bikes, which soon gained their own immortality as "choppers."

These bikes were the opposite of the decked-out FLHs that had long been Harley-Davidson's bread and butter, and fundamentally different from the slightly stripped "bobbers" of previous decades, too. First of all, choppers weren't stripped to make them lighter for racing or to give them the racer look. Instead, choppers were stripped and cut and molded purely for style—more specifically to set them apart from Dad's old "decked" FLH.

Fenders weren't just bobbed; they were sometimes thrown away altogether. Same with the other practical features Harley built into its big Electra Glide—like front brakes, cushy balloon tires, electric starters, and shock absorbers. In their places sprouted skinny, 19- and 21-inch front tires, wildly extended forks, tiny "peanut" and coffin tanks, sissy bars, stepped saddles, hardtail frames, and chrome on anything made of metal.

Choppers got more extreme and decadent with each passing year, until the average guy just couldn't keep up. After all, not everyone's a welder or sheet-metal bender or custom painter—or could afford to pay the kind of money the professional chopper builders were beginning to charge.

Here was a rare opportunity to win over a whole new generation of customers, either by building the parts or by offering factory-built versions of the Harleys these guys wanted. Did Harley-Davidson seize the moment? Not until it was almost too late, unfortunately. Harley-Davidson and most of its dealers were more conservative than John Birchers and of one mind on the chopper issue. If you want a new Electra Glide or some extra lights or saddlebags to hang on it, "Come on in!" If you want a tall sissy bar or a 10-inch-over fork, "Get the hell out of my dealership, kid!"

Snubbed by the Motor Company, the chopper boys saw no need to buy new bikes, either. Instead, they bought cast-off Knuckleheads and Panheads as the basis for their choppers, and an entrepreneurial few among them kick-started a whole new industry to produce chopper parts such as tanks, sissy bars, abbreviated fenders, custom wheels, and even hardtail frames for those whose starting point was one of the more recent Harleys with rear suspension.

The original Softail of 1984 was the first factory chopper. Harley-Davidson took that chopper look back another generation with the Springer of 1988.

Why hardtails, when everyone knew they were uncomfortable and handled horribly? The answer is that the chopper boys were even more conservative on one issue of style than the Motor Company itself. Sure, mile-long forks, upswept pipes, and mast-tall sissy bars were essential parts of chopper styling, but so was a styling element that you could only get (then) with a hardtail frame. That styling element was what many call "the line," and it was almost as old as the Motor Company itself.

To understand the essence of the look they were after, you have to look back to Harley's first real styling masterpiece, the 1936 Model E, commonly known as the "Knucklehead." This bike introduced the classic Harley teardrop saddle tanks and "the line." That combination made it arguably the best-looking Harley ever built and certainly the most stylistically influential.

What's "the line"?

It's the way the rear frame rails extend the top line of the Knuckle's teardrop tanks all the way back to the rear axle. That line and the way it extended the teardrop of the tank were the hallmarks of the Big Twin look from 1936 until Harley broke it by adding a swingarm and rear shocks to turn the Hydra-Glide into the Duo-Glide.

Even though Harley-Davidson abandoned "the line," the chopper boys never did. That clean look to the rear end was more important to them than practical considerations such as road holding and ride—more important even than the health of their own irreplaceable vertebrae. You saw it on the choppers in *Easy Rider* and all over the street once the custom movement broke into the mainstream, and it has been carried forward to this day as an essential styling element of the best-looking customs—and any number of Harley knock-offs from Japan.

But for every guy who accepted all the consequences to have that clean, uncluttered look to his bike's rear end, there were 10,000 who wished they didn't have to. They wanted "the line" without risking their spine.

Several small aftermarket manufacturers soon attempted to cash in on the desire for a soft-on-the-spine hardtail. Most of them used variations of the old "plunger-style" rear suspension (in which only the axle was sprung). These didn't work very well as suspension. Worse, they didn't look like a hardtail, either, so plunger frames soon faded back into history. (As an aside, one of these ill-fated systems was even marketed as the "Softail," for a time.)

One man had a better idea. He designed a system that used a triangular swingarm to get the line, but with shock absorbers mounted under the transmission to soak up the jolts. Harley-Davidson quickly noted the potential and put that faux hardtail into production as the 1984 FXST Softail.

Some reviewers, of course, criticized the Softail for its lack of ground clearance, stiff ride, and way-forward controls. Most saw it for what it was, however: "It's not a motorcycle, baby, it's a factory chopper." And they recognized that if they had to grade the Softail on a curve for function, they also had to grade every other factory motorcycle on a curve for style.

Harley's factory chopper proved to be exactly what those thousands of get-the-line-without-breaking-your-spine chopper aficionados really wanted. It outsold all the other big Harleys its first year and brought in critical profits at a time when Harley-Davidson was constantly just an overadvance away from bankruptcy.

The Softail's runaway success powered Harley-Davidson back into solvency, drove Harley's competitors to the sincerest form of flattery, and started a renaissance that eventually saw Harley-Davidson become the number one seller of streetbikes in the U.S. market. We'll get to all that soon enough. For now, let's move on and meet the man who started it all.

ONE

BILL DAVIS AND THE DESIGN OF THE FIRST SOFTAIL

"I loved the custom hardtail look . . . so I decided to build one for myself."

—Bill Davis, designer of the Softail

Our tale begins not inside the hallowed halls of Harley-Davidson, nor even in Milwaukee, but inside a biker's garage in Missouri.

Bill Davis, an avid rider, customizer, and mechanical engineer from the St. Louis, Missouri, area was unhappy with the looks of his 1972 Super Glide and started sketching out plans for customizing the Glide into the kind of Harley he really wanted. "I loved the custom hardtail look," said Davis, "but my interest was in long trips, so I couldn't live with the horrid, uncomfortable ride of the rigid."

Aftermarket manufacturers at the time offered several frames claiming to give hardtail looks along with swingarm-and-shocks comfort. "They were all making plunger designs [on which only the rear axle was sprung]," explained Davis. "They didn't look very efficient to me, and they didn't look like a rigid, either. I thought there had to be a better way, so I decided to build one for myself."

Building Softail One

Davis began to experiment with several different suspension configurations on his Super Glide in 1974–75. Before long, he had settled on the key piece that gave him the hardtail profile and true suspension: a triangular swingarm with the pivot on a vertical member between the upper and lower arms.

Though his swingarm design was similar in concept to the suspensions used on the Vincent Rapides and Black Shadows of the 1940s and Yamaha dirt bikes of the 1970s, Davis' reasons for using it were the opposite of theirs. Function was the driving force for both Vincent and Yamaha, so both companies flaunted their rear suspension. Davis was after hardtail style, so his design was complicated somewhat by the need to hide the fact that it really *was* suspension. Cleverly, Davis hid under the seat the twin springs and single snowmobile shock that provided suspension. The frame and undercarriage hid the swingarm pivot.

Opposite: Visionary, though he was, Softail inventor Bill Davis could never have guessed how far Harley would take the concept or how successful it would be.

To carry forward the line from the swingarm and complete the hardtail look, Davis bent his Super Glide's frame rails down so they lined up with the top rails of the swingarm. The final piece was a custom oil tank to mimic the look of the underseat horseshoe oil tanks of the Knuckleheads and Pans.

So successfully did Davis' modified Super Glide (he hadn't yet named the suspension system) capture the hardtail look that "only people who really knew Harleys could tell there was suspension at all," said Davis. "It looked really, really good. Others have told me that my prototype was the best looking of them all. I raked out the front end and put on 10-inch-over forks and custom triple-trees. And I took off the AMF decals. It looked more like a hardtail chopper than any that came after because of all the hand work that went into it."

Davis' prototype had the hardtail chopper look all right, but he still wasn't satisfied because the seat was too high and the oil tank didn't look quite right. After some

refinement, he got the seat height low enough and the oil tank just right.

When he was done, Davis did what came naturally: he proudly rode it all around. "It performed very well," he remembered, "but the springs were too soft. I replaced them with heavier ones, and it was perfect." So he took it on long trips. Everywhere he went, "people who really knew Harleys told me how much they loved it." We'll call this historic machine Softail One.

Because people loved it, Davis began to think of building and selling copies. He hired a patent attorney and filed patents on the design. It didn't take him long to realize that it would be easier and cheaper to sell custom-built frames with his new suspension than it would be to develop bolt-on suspension kits, so he began work on refining the frame for production.

Harley's First Look

While Davis was in the midst of all that, he thought up an even better idea: Why not show his prototype to Harley? He picked up

Bill Davis' first aftermarket frame design for Harley-Davidson Big Twins. *Bill Davis*

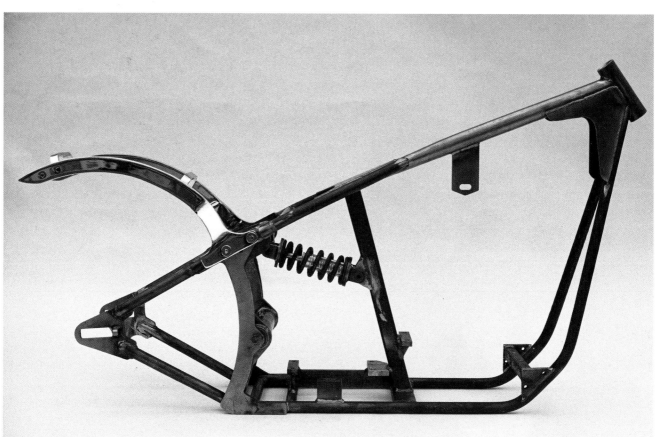

the phone, dialed Harley's number, and asked for Willie G. "In those days, they'd put you right through," he remembered. Willie G. seemed receptive, so they arranged a meeting.

"I rode the bike up to Milwaukee accompanied by a friend who had just bought a Gold Wing," Davis remembered. "It was August 1976, and it was hot!" After going inside the Juneau Avenue plant and meeting with Louie Netz (Willie G.'s right-hand man in Styling), Davis and his friend escorted Netz and some engineers outside to see Davis' faux hardtail. The prototype was so custom that one engineer asked, "Is there anything Harley on here?" remembered Davis. Later, Willie G. came down, too.

"They were very impressed," remembered Davis, "but they didn't really make any commitments. I didn't hear from them again

until about six months later. I got a letter from Willie G. that said, 'Our engineering slate's full right now, but we *are* interested.'"

Davis didn't just wait around for Willie G. to call, however. "After that," Davis continued, "I figured, maybe I can make it myself. So I continued to improve the design to make it easier to manufacture. It would have been a mess to make the new frames like the one on my prototype." After building jigs and fixtures, Davis cranked out "six to ten" frames for other customizers in the St. Louis area. While building the frames, he devised a way to further lower the seat height by using twin shocks (still under the seat, but parallel to the frame rails) and a new oil tank that got him closer to the look he was after. He built "about a dozen" of these frames and even designed and built a similar frame for Sportsters.

Call this bike Softail One—Bill Davis' first iteration of what became the Softail rear end was built onto his customized 1972 Super Glide, shown here. *Bill Davis*

Road Worx

While Davis worked to refine his faux hardtail for production, he eked out a living by building custom parts and stretching and raking frames for others in the area. One day, a guy brought his Knucklehead to Davis for some frame work. While at Davis' shop, the Knuckle guy saw Davis' new design, immediately saw its potential, and began talking Davis into forming a partnership to make and market the frame.

"He was a sales guy, almost mesmerizing, real good with business and people," said Davis. "Really, he was the perfect complement for my personality. When I agreed, he just took the ball and really ran with it." (Davis prefers not to give his former partner's name, so let's call him the "Business Guy," "BG" for short.)

Run with it, he did. First, the BG did marketing studies and sent out questionnaires within the industry to test the market. Then, he arranged a loan to start the business while Davis continued refining the design for production and building tooling. Before long, they'd set up a shop and selected a company name: Road Worx.

During all this, Harley-Davidson called. This time it was Jeff Bleustein (then Harley's vice president of engineering, now CEO). Bleustein liked the concept and advocated for it within the company. He told Davis that Harley was still very interested in making an offer for the design, so Davis journeyed to Milwaukee to discuss the offer. To Davis, Harley's offer seemed "lowball." After consulting with his lawyer, Davis asked for more. Harley then upped the offer, but not enough to change his mind.

An Inspired Breakthrough: the "Sub Shock"

Returning home disappointed once again, Davis continued working on the last real

Here's how he got it. His first system used the triangular swingarm shown, along with a snowmobile shock absorber and twin springs up under the seat. *Bill Davis*

problem with the design: he kept having to raise the seat to keep the springs from scraping on the seat pan. He tried several ideas before true inspiration struck.

"In desperation, almost," remembered Davis, "I figured out a way to fit the shocks underneath the tranny. It was really tight, but that solved all my problems with seat height and using a really good-looking horseshoe oil tank." (As an aside, motorcycles with under-engine springs or shocks had also been tried in the past, even by Harley-Davidson, on the Model BH Scat of 1963.)

Unfortunately, it also created formidable new challenges. "All the shocks that I knew of at that time operated in compression," he said. "But my system required shocks to operate in tension. And I didn't have much room because if the shocks were too large, they'd bottom out on the road." He ended up making the "shocks" out of cylinders of polyurethane, a polymer that served as both spring and damper because the material is self-damping by nature.

Davis quickly built a prototype frame with the improved rear end and dressed it up like the most chopperesque Harley of the day, the FXWG Wide Glide. Then he began road-testing it and the polyurethane shocks. Many miles and subtle refinements later, he was finally satisfied with their performance. And he thought up a name for it: "Sub Shock." Even neater and cleaner than the Softail One system, the Sub Shock design also featured innovations such as belt drive and Teflon-lined spherical swingarm bearings.

On to Sturgis

Hoping the new Sub Shock would create a stir among the tens of thousands of Harley faithful gathered at Sturgis, South Dakota, Davis and the BG headed there in early August 1980 on Softail One (built on a 1972 Super Glide) and the first Sub Shock bike.

All those miles of road testing had perfected the Sub Shock mechanism, but the road trip to Sturgis revealed a materials problem that Davis hadn't anticipated.

Here are the shock and springs. This arrangement worked well, but the shock and springs took up the room under the seat that Davis wanted for a horseshoe oil tank and forced a higher seat height than he wanted. On this version, he used the vertical oil tank shown on the left side of the bike. *Bill Davis*

Heat building up in the enclosed shocks was gradually breaking down the polyurethane, so the cylinders began to take a "set." As a result, the Sub Shock bike began riding lower and lower on its suspension and acting more and more like a real hardtail.

Davis and the BG decided to hold off on showing the new Sub Shock, for two reasons—most immediately because they weren't sure the shocks would make it all the way to Sturgis, but also because the BG thought it was dangerous to show the design before they had gotten the patents on it. The BG steered the Sub Shock bike back toward St. Louis,

while Davis went on to South Dakota on Softail One. Further misfortune struck once Davis reached Deadwood, when a bunch of his stuff was stolen from his saddlebags. Disgusted, Davis headed for home without ever showing either bike at Sturgis.

Springing Back

Davis didn't let those misfortunes sidetrack him. After riding home from Sturgis, he began work on new springs and dampers to replace the failed polyurethane units. "I realized I had to use the tried-and-true metal spring and oil-damper system for the shock absorber," he recalled. "Still, there wasn't much room for the springs, so I ended up using die springs. [Die springs are super-heavy-duty springs used in industrial presses that give high spring rates in a very small package.] They're powerful and are designed to stand up to lots of cycles, but they're also expensive."

Davis needed tiny springs because the under-tranny space he had for the shocks was so small that the springs would have to be enclosed within the damper housing. "I had to assemble them under pressure, holding it all together in a press while I welded the housings," Davis explained. "It was an expensive shock to build." He also had to make them function in tension rather than compression, as did every other shock in the world. "I had to design my own special pistons and valving to get them to work right," he explained.

At this point the Sub Shock design was almost ready for production, so Davis and the BG took on another partner, a mechanic and fabricator who would help build the tooling and produce the frames. "He was a real asset to the company," remembered Davis. He and Davis then designed and built the production tooling, while the BG sent out the final promotional flurry, including the purchase of a full-page ad in the April 1981 *Easyriders* magazine. The ad showed the Sub Shock frame and a Wide Glide fitted with it. Looking at that bike, it's easy to see how little the styling was really changed for the production Harley Softail.

Falling Apart Again

Even before that *Easyriders* ad came out, the Road Worx partnership began to unravel. Most of the discord came from the BG, who began to chafe under the mundane routine of running the office. "It turned out that all

the fun was over for him once the business was set up," remembered Davis.

All the promotion was showing signs of success, though, as orders came in for 21 frames. Pulling together one last time, the Road Worx crew constructed the frames and shipped them off. During the process, Davis and the BG realized that they could no longer work together, so they dissolved the partnership. "You can't believe the pain and horror he put me through. He turned the whole thing into living hell."

Road Worx was defunct, but Davis was still on the hook for the company's business loans. His lawyers advised him to sell the idea to another manufacturer. Reluctant to "crawl back" (Davis' words) to Harley-Davidson, he approached several aftermarket builders, an investment group, and even Honda. American Honda returned his proposal with a letter saying they didn't accept unsolicited ideas. The aftermarket and investment groups all made scandalously low offers for the design. "I was so naive!" he said of the experience. "I almost lost the rights to my patents to some of those sharks. Everybody wanted a piece of me."

Before Harley bought the design, Davis began selling aftermarket versions of his frame. Here, Davis is shown with six frames he built with a revised, twin-shock design and "wishbone" downtubes for even more of the 1940s look. *Bill Davis*

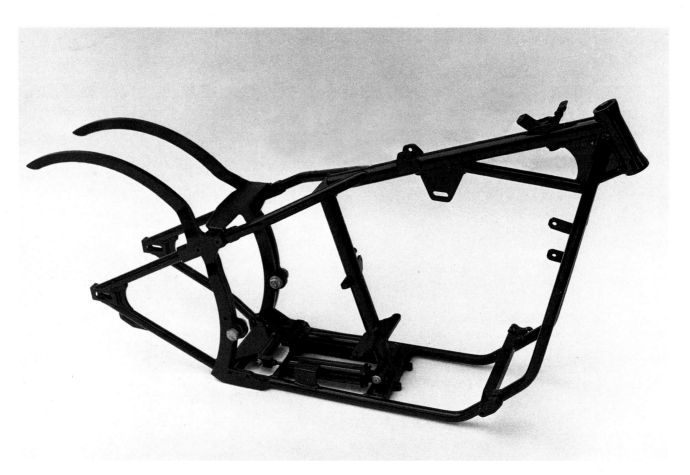

After several revisions on the basic design, Davis hit upon the idea that made the whole hardtail look possible: he put the shocks under the transmission and designed them to work in extension rather than by compression. The shocks shown are actually made of urethane, which acts as both spring and damper but didn't last as long as Davis had hoped. After that, he designed more conventional hydraulically damped shocks and began advertising the frame as the "Sub Shock." *Bill Davis*

Harley-Davidson to the Rescue

Out of better options, his head "just swimming from all the deception," Davis decided to "crawl back" and gave Harley's Jeff Bleustein a call. "He was still interested and made a much, much better offer." Davis consulted his lawyers. Even they thought the deal looked good, but there was a catch.

Harley offered Davis a royalty on each unit sold. That was the good part. The bad part was that Harley proposed a lifetime cap on total royalty earnings. Davis objected to the cap, but Bleustein wouldn't budge, insisting that Harley chief Vaughn Beals was adamant that Harley would only pay up to that amount, no matter how many units were sold.

"I didn't like the idea of the cap when we were negotiating the agreement," remem-bered Davis, "but my patent attorney told me, 'Take it; the royalties will never get there.'" Another consideration weighed on Davis and his lawyers: "My patent was kind of weak," he admitted. "We were worried that Harley-Davidson would build it anyway if we didn't agree to the deal." Davis relented and signed the deal on January 6, 1982, selling Harley the Sub Shock Wide Glide prototype, the patents for the design, all the tooling, and six complete Sub Shock frames.

The excitement of striking a deal was over, and Davis immersed himself in finding work to keep financially afloat until he started receiving royalties from Harley. At first, he went back to customizing bikes again, while seeking additional design work. "Remember, I was out of a job [when Road Worx folded] and in debt," he empha-

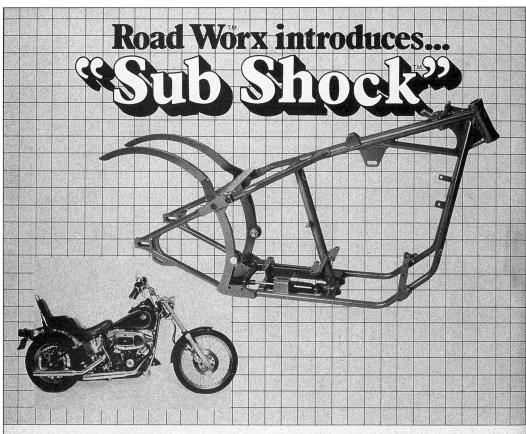

Here's the one big ad run by Davis and his partners in *Easyriders*. Note that, like the Softail Harley built on the idea, the Sub Shock bike is based on a Wide Glide and even has the chromed horseshoe oil tank. The swingarm pivots have Teflon spherical bearings, similar to those later used on production Softails.
Bill Davis

sized. "Mr. Bleustein had promised me more projects but they never called again until after I finally took a job with a medical company to make ends meet. At first, I designed opthalmic ultrasound scanning probes. Later, we got into urological ultrasound equipment, and I designed the world's first ultrasound probe that was able to selectively scan the prostate in two mutually perpendicular planes."

The Production Softail

Busy as he was, Davis didn't think much more about his design until one day about a year and a half year later when a friend showed him a picture in a maga-

An aftermarket frame Bill Davis designed for Harley's XL-Series engines. *Bill Davis*

zine of an all-new Harley model that looked an awful lot like the Sub Shock Wide Glide from the *Easyriders* ad. It was, of course, the production FXST Softail, which made its debut along with Harley's new Evolution engine in the summer of 1983, as a 1984 model.

"The first thing I noticed was that they'd changed the shape of the fender supports," Davis remembered. "Mine were curved in an arc, concentric with the wheel. For style reasons, Willie G. had made them straight and parallel with the line of the mufflers. I thought mine looked better."

Was Davis exhilarated that his hard-fought battle to get the hardtail look to market had succeeded on such a grand scale? Not really. The pain was still too fresh, you might say. "I'd gone through such

horror with that guy [the BG] that I wasn't excited about anything," he explained. "I didn't love it anymore; I just didn't care."

He began to care when he finally saw a Softail for real. With a creative engineer's singular brand of insecurity, he'd long wondered how good his basic design really was. What would need changing for mass production and to please everyone at a big company like Harley? Would they validate all the choices and trade-offs he had made or would they scrap much of it and make different choices? To his delight, Harley hadn't made fundamental changes to the design. "They designed their own coil-over shocks and bearings and such, but the tri-angulation and all the rest were basically the same," he observed. "I felt it confirmed my engineering ability."

From the day of its introduction, the Softail was the new star of the Harley lineup. Despite its premium price, it outsold all the other Big Twin Harleys and brought in much-needed profits to the nearly bankrupt Motor Company. Harley was happy with its deal, and soon Davis was too, as the royalties started rolling in.

Harley-Davidson quickly added new Softail models, and they all sold well, too, such that those royalties kept coming and coming. Eventually, against all odds, the amount reached the lifetime cap. Nevertheless, Davis is anything but bitter. "Of course, if that cap wasn't there, I wouldn't have to work today," he said, "but Harley's treatment of me was the only shining part of the story; the rest was just hell."

Although he no longer receives royalties, the company makes it up to him by keeping him busy with a number of freelance engineering projects—some of which you may soon see at your local Harley-Davidson dealer.

Here's the Sub Shock Wide Glide from the ad. Except for the Shovelhead motor, curved fender supports, and old ham-can air cleaner, this could pass for a 1984 production Softail. *Bill Davis*

TWO

THE FX SOFTAIL MODELS, 1984–1999

"That's gonna be the best-selling Harley-Davidson ever!"

—Harley CEO Vaughn Beals on seeing the prototype Softail

Just as the MoCo's engineers began modifying Bill Davis' Sub Shock prototype into a production model, the Harley-Davidson Motor Company began to founder in its own perfect storm.

"A semi-recession had hit automotive earlier," explained Tom Gelb, former vice president of operations, "and all of a sudden in March of '82 it hit us. At the time, the Japanese motorcycle manufacturers had about 18 months' worth of finished inventory in this country, and they were selling two- and three-year-old bikes right out of the crate and discounting them, so the bottom fell out of the market. I remember we had a policy meeting, and in the next weeks we cut our production rate in half, laid off 40 percent of our workforce, and cut all the wages of the officers by something like 12 percent and the salaried workforce by 10 percent."

What Harley really needed to pull itself out of this hole was a hip new model, and

CEO Vaughn Beals and a few others were sure they had it in the Sub Shock. He predicted, "That's gonna be the best-selling Harley-Davidson ever!" in a Product Planning Committee meeting. "The Softail was a dynamite concept," he explained. "It just takes the vehicle back a whole generation. The Japanese don't have that heritage, but we do. It gave us something we could do that was unique."

Marketing was even more hot to trot, according to now-retired vice president of engineering Mark Tuttle: "Marketing saw that motorcycle [Davis' Sub Shock, figuring it was complete and ready for production] and said, 'Hey great, we can have this in six months!'

"What they didn't realize was that all we had was a very good concept that still had to be refined and validated. We said, 'No, you can't have it in six months. We've got to design all these new parts and test them; it's gonna take three years or something.'

Opposite: The 1984 Softail was a chopper for the masses—and as good a piece of chopper art as most of the one-off customs of the day. Combining chopper looks with the modern functionality of the Evolution motor, the Softail became Harley's best seller in 1984, then split and split again into a whole range of new models that topped the sales charts.

Conceived in the mind of independent engineer Bill Davis and given birth in Milwaukee, the FXST Softail was an instant hit when released for model year 1984.

"Of course, they said that was totally unacceptable, so we set up a focus team—handpicked people with Ron Hutchinson in charge to launch the product in as short a time as possible."

Team Softail

That handpicked team integrated Engineering's efforts with those of Styling and Marketing to try to cut the three-year birthing process in half, with the goal of introducing the new model for 1984. Hutchinson and his team sequestered themselves in their own separate space to foster quick work and close cooperation.

For the purposes of this book, we'll call them Team Softail.

Despite the time pressures, Team Softail's engineers spent considerable effort to refine the Sub Shock. They used computer modeling and structural-engineering tricks to stiffen it and worked closely with Styling to get the look right. Before long, it was ready for testing and further refinement, both of which progressed rapidly because of team coordination.

For Bill Davis—a one-man operation—the laid-down, under-tranny shocks had been more problematical than any other component. For Harley-Davidson,

Though the Softail's rear end looked rigid, the new machine featured a hidden suspension using the triangular swingarm shown here and twin shocks underneath the transmission.

they were no big deal. According to Mark Tuttle, "We were able to go to our shock manufacturer with an envelope of load curves and say, 'We need a shock that fits in this space, with these spring and damping rates,' and we let them do the rest. That's the benefit the factory has. We can call on someone who has that specific expertise to develop the component for us."

In this case, that someone was the Japanese suspension manufacturer Showa, which had started building XL and FX forks for Harley-Davidson in the 1970s and had gradually been taking over all of Harley's suspension business. Because the new shocks laid flat and extended as the suspension compressed, they were a challenge even for Showa. Nevertheless, remembered Booth, "Showa jumped into the Softail project and came up with gas-charged shocks that worked pretty well."

The Whole Hardtail Look

Styling's goal for the production machine was nothing less than "the whole hardtail look," according to one team member. That meant more than hiding shocks and pivot points; it meant recapturing the clean styling of the early Harleys. A key piece in

that was in re-creating the line—the flowing line from the top of the gas tanks all the way back to the rear axle—to recapture the slim look of the Knucklehead. Willie G. and Team Softail followed Davis' lead and got the look they were after.

Another key part of the look was the classic horseshoe oil tank, with the battery nestled in the "U" of the horseshoe. Harley's engineers worried that the heat from the oil tank would damage the battery. But the horseshoe tank was an essential part of the look and there was no other good place for the battery, so they developed a battery that could take the heat and do the job.

Since sprung "tractor" seats were no longer in fashion in the early 1980s, the new oil tank was fitted with a filler spout on its right side because the Softail's frame-mounted seat covered up the traditional top-mounted filler.

For the rest of the styling, Willie G. and his partner in Styling, Louie Netz, did what Davis had done in building the Sub Shock bike shown in the *Easyriders* ad (see chapter 1): they reprised the chopper style of the FXWG Wide Glide. Like the Softail, the Wide Glide was another great

The rest of the Softail's look was chopperesque, with the wide, extended forks of the Wide Glide. Its spindly looking, wide-spaced forks emulated the look customizers had been creating for decades by stripping the shrouds off the Hydra-Glide fork, turning down the sliders on a lathe, extending the fork tubes, lacing up a skinny 21-inch rim, adding a small bullet headlight, and chroming everything.

idea Harley-Davidson plucked from the aftermarket. That look originally came from stripping off the headlight and fork covers from the standard Hydra-Glide front end, substituting longer fork tubes and a smaller headlight, and lathe-turning the sliders for a slimmer look. Substitute a slim, 21-inch front wheel and a "bikini" fender, and the whole front end has that slim, wide-spaced look, "wide glide" in chopper lingo. Chopper guys had been doing it themselves for years, but, according to Vaughn Beals, a southern California dealer also got in on the act. He began building and selling them as "Wide Glides" for several years before Harley did it. "These were high-mileage California police bikes," said Beals, "and he was selling the damn things for about the same price as a brand-new Harley. I figured people must want one badly to pay that. We decided that the Wide Glide would be a hell

of a good bike to produce. The head of Marketing and I were the only guys, I think, that believed it, though. We had to beat the rest of them up to do it."

Most notable at first glance was the Softail's Wide Glide front-end look: a skinny, 21-inch, wire-spoked front wheel with chrome rim; a severely chopped front fender; a single front disc brake; a tiny chromed headlight; and chromed triple clamps. As a concession to both style and comfort, the Wide Glide's tall, chromed handlebar risers were tweaked back a bit before being bolted to the Softail. The Softail's speedo was mounted on the tank-top console, leaving those bars clean and instrument-free.

Willie and Louie also graced the Softail with the Wide Glide's 5-gallon "Mega Bob" tanks, which accentuated the slim, wide-spaced look of the Wide Glide front end.

Right: The beating heart of Harley's new Softail was the new-for-'84 Evolution engine. The new Evolution motor looked new and old at the same time. New for 1984 was a return to the classic round air cleaner used from 1937 until it was abandoned in the 1970s in favor of the larger, quieter "ham-can" air cleaners of the late AMF era.

Below: With the Softail, Harley brought back "the line"— continuous from the top of the speedo console all the way back to the rear axle—and the whole look of the chopped Harleys built on the old hardtail frames of 1936–57.

Harley fitted the old dual saddle tanks and the tank-mounted speedo, a styling treatment dating back to the first of the "modern" Harley Big Twins, the 61 OHV "Knucklehead" of 1936. Tanks on the Softail were the 5-gallon version of the Fat Bob tanks, first used on the 1965 Electra Glide. For 1984 only, the Softail was fitted with the federally mandated 85-mph speedometer.

They affixed the grand old Harley bar-and-shield emblem, in gold, on the side of each tank. For that first year, they would offer Vivid Black or Candy Red paint, each with gold pinstripes.

At the rear they fitted the Wide Glide's bobbed fender, with taillight and strut-mounted license-plate bracket underneath. Atop that fender they bolted a seat unique to the new model. Deeply stepped and thinly padded, the seat that soon earned the "clamshell" moniker gave the lowest seat height of any big bike: 25.3 inches, according to H-D specs. Quipped *Cycle* magazine

Befitting a new classic, the 1984 Softail tanks were fitted with classic gold Harley-Davidson bar-and-shield emblems.

Buckhorn bars on tall risers added to the chopper look.

(February 1985), "If seats get much lower than this one, tall riders will be able to plant both knees firmly on the ground at stoplights."

The Softail wasn't just a looker, either. It was powered by the shiny, new aluminum Evolution engine, rigidly mounted to trans-fer that familiar Harley throb straight from motor mounts to frame to rider. No rubber in the drive, either—chains for both primary and final. The tranny was traditional, too. Four speeds, kickstarter and all. Filling the engine V on the right was a round air

For 1984, the Softail was the only Evo-engined Harley with a kickstarter.

cleaner (after years of those huge, hideous ham-can air cleaners), just like on the old Harleys. A shorty dual exhaust helped complete the chopper look.

Ready for Prime Time

Less than a year and a half after buying Bill Davis' Sub Shock design, Harley-Davidson proudly introduced the production version, the FXST Softail, to the motorcycling press in June 1983, as a 1984 model. Predictably, the "biker" press (*Easyriders*, *Supercycle*, and all) loved it. So did their readers. Better yet for a company that was looking to break out of the mold, the more mainstream press gave it their begrudging admiration, too.

The Evolution engine was supposed to have been the star at the press introduction, but the Softail was so novel and looked so good that it stole the show. Harley reps had to keep steering attention back to the merits of the Evo engine and to the other updates to the whole 1984 line, while everyone congregated around Harley's badass new factory chop.

The Softail was all about style, but it all worked well enough that even editors who month after month fawned over the latest Interceptors and imitation Harleys from Japan couldn't fault it too much. At "55 mph the vibes are pretty tolerable," wrote the editors of *Cycle* magazine in the January 1984 issue. Of course, they couldn't resist a clever cut that, because of those vibes, "The four-speed 80-incher is one of the most effective speed-limitation devices known to mankind." Nevertheless, those same editors acknowledged the FXST's essential appeal, calling it "a rolling picture frame for the individual rider." And who among Harley's traditionalist fans couldn't picture themselves there?

Even better, Harley's new "rolling picture frame" was so gilded that scads of non-traditionalists could also imagine themselves sitting there—vibes or not. That this rolling frame was more handsome than most of its riders was the point entirely and a sincere tribute to the skills of Willie and Louie, and Bill Davis, too. That it also felt and sounded right was testament to the fact that everyone at Harley pulled together to get the other intangibles right.

At $7,999, the Softail was more expensive than any other non-bagger Harley. Despite that, it went on to outsell everything else in the Harley Big Twin line in its first year, proving the foresight of Beals and Bleustein and the other believers. Even better for the cash-strapped Motor Company, the Softail's success was won without cutting notably into the net sales of the other Big Twins.

Softail's success fueled a 31 percent rise in Harley's domestic sales, to 38,741—a phenomenal increase in a year in which the U.S. motorcycle market accelerated deeper and deeper into a death spin that would continue through the 1980s. Yamaha, for example, lost an astonishing $150 million in the United States for the year ending April 30, 1984, as it dumped thousands of Visions and XS650s for a fraction of retail. To put Yamaha's loss in perspective, it's nearly twice what Beals and friends had paid for the Harley-Davidson Motor

Company in June 1981. (Ominously for Harley, though, the only bike Yamaha had no trouble selling that year was the Harley-style Virago, which was selling so quickly that some of the magazines couldn't even get one to test.)

Best of all, according to Vaughn Beals, was, "Once we had the Softail, we could do all kinds of wondrous things with it." And before long, they did.

Forward controls, a deeply stepped seat, and high bars gave the Softail a chopper's stretched-out, laid-back ride.

1985 Softails

Harley's factory chopper was back for 1985, with few changes. The marquee change was

Harley-Davidson made two notable changes for 1985: the "winged ball" tank graphics shown here, and belt rear drive.

to belt final drive. (Interestingly, Bill Davis' Sub Shock had featured belt drive, but Harley-Davidson reverted to a rear chain for the first-year production Softail.)

Like all the 1985 Harleys, the Softail came with a diaphram-spring wet clutch (this had been a running change in mid-1984) and a bunch of other minor updates. Another update might seem minor, but it meant a lot to some motorcyclists because it gave them hope that the fuel- and safety-Nazis wouldn't always win: Harley-Davidson fitted a 120-mph speedometer to replace the 85-mph unit that had been mandatory since the late 1970s. The Softail couldn't really push the limits of a 120-mph speedo, but gearheads across the fruited plain cheered the return of real speedometers anyway.

Softail tanks were graced with beautiful eagle-wing tank transfers for 1985, encircled by a double pinstripe. Tanks were also uprated to 5.2 gallons (from 5 gallons). Paint options were Vivid Black, Candy Red, and Candy Blue. For extra cost, Softy was available in Candy Burgundy with Slate Gray panels. For those not satisfied with Willie G.'s choice of colors, Harley offered its custom paint program, allowing customers to order a new machine painted in any color or combination in the Harley catalogs.

All those updates came at a cost. Harley raised the Softail's price $400, to $8,399. Despite the price increase, Softail sales rose.

Bigger changes were in store for 1986. Shown here is one of them: the FXSTC Softail Custom, a new upscale version of the Softail.

Five-Speeds and the FXSTC Softail Custom

Harley's four-speed transmission was a 1930s design that was very expensive and labor-intensive to manufacture, so for 1986 the Softail's frame was revised to carry the five-speed transmission used by the rest of the line. Harley's chassis engineers took the opportunity to make the five-speed Softail frame stiffer, easier to manufacture, and better looking, all at the same time. The major change was to a stout new forging to replace the flame-cut curved piece on each side that bridges the upper and lower frame

The Custom really was: two-tone paint on the tanks and fenders, chrome-and-black engine, frame painted Candy Burgundy to match tanks and fenders, and many other details.

rails at the rear. "It was a beautiful piece," explained former Harley engineer Rit Booth, "if you like sculptured steel."

Harley's five-speed transmission was designed without provision for a kickstarter, so the 1986 Softails gave up that macho link to the past. Many mourned (and still do) the loss of this backup starting system. "We had a major insurrection over

that," remembered Beals, but the company decided, "The hell with it" and just ignored the complaints.

There were other minor changes, too, including updated tank emblems and tuned intakes and exhaust to make them comply with government noise standards. The Softail still had its old feel, though, because even though the 1986 Softail got the

five-speed and a revised frame, rubber mounts weren't part of the formula.

The five-speed Softail sold even better than the four-speed, even though the price for the basic Softail was up to $8,749. By the end of the year, there was a waiting list in many parts of the country for the Softail—another look into Harley's future.

FXSTC Softail Custom

One of the keys to Harley's resurgence in the 1980s and dominance of the U.S. big-bike market in the 1990s was in the way it was able to add more and more chrome and custom touches to create premium-priced Custom versions of its basic models.

This practice all began with the limited-edition FXRDG Disc Glide of 1984, which was the first of many Harley glitter wagons to come. Harley-Davidson's marketing department saw gold in equipping Harleys with more and more chrome from the factory. Unfortunately, the process for chroming aluminum castings, in production-line quantities, day in and day out, was far more difficult than anyone realized. Hoping to perfect the process, while minimizing the risks of slowing down regular production, Harley's management decided that they'd experiment with a few limited-edition chromed models and gradually spread the chrome across the model line.

The Disc Glide was the first of these with the Evo engine. It was given 12 chromed covers on its engine (including timer, starter, valve covers, primary, tranny top and side) that really gave the engine a more refined, custom, and finished look. Everyone (even magazine reviewers) who

In 1986, the frame and swingarm were revised to stiffen the assembly and to fit a five-speed transmission. One of the most visible parts of the redesign is the new frame forging shown here just ahead of the passenger peg. On 1984 and 1985 Softails, a less-sculptured flame-cut piece was used instead of the forging.

Right: Tanks and fenders were painted Candy Burgundy with Candy Red panels. The scroll tank graphics shown here were unique to the Softail Custom.

Below: The Custom also featured an aluminum disc rear wheel.

saw it commented on how much the chrome improved the looks of the engine.

The key to getting chrome for the whole model line was in getting its suppliers to eliminate hidden flaws and porosity in the aluminum castings and then to get its chrome platers to increase capacity. In 1985 came the FXRC and primped versions of the FLT and FLHT. Through that strategy, Harley was finally able to get up to speed enough to offer chromed and blacked-out engines on regular-production models.

By 1986 Harley was confident enough in their processes to release the FXSTC Softail Custom, which was the first of what would soon be a long line of chrome-encrusted, regular-production "Custom" models. Crinkle black finish was painted on the Softail Custom's crankcases, cylinders, cylinder heads, and transmission case, all highlighted with polished cooling-fin ends, chrome rocker-box covers, chrome outer primary, and chrome transmission covers.

Except for the chrome-and-black engine, the most notable features of the Softail Custom were its disc-type rear wheel and a frame painted (all the others were powdercoated) Candy Burgundy to match

the two-tone Candy Burgundy and Candy Red paint on the tanks. Add on the new "pillowy" seat, sissy bar, and special scroll tank graphics, and this off-the-rack Harley showed more style than the majority of one-off customs did. All that for $9,299, only $500 more than for the standard Softail. Despite the higher price, the Softail Custom outsold not only its less-expensive and plainer brother, but every other Harley Big Twin, as well.

Midway through the model year, Harley introduced yet another slice of Softail, the FLST Heritage Softail, which flaunted a fat front end styled after those of the 1950s Hydra-Glides. It, too, soon split

Harley-Davidson developed the processes for chrome plating engine covers in production-line quantities by using them on a series of limited-edition chrome-encrusted specials in 1984 and 1985. By 1986 the company was ready to put all that chrome on the regular-production Softail Custom. It was Harley's best-selling Big Twin that year.

to form its own model line. Read all about it in chapter 3.

The 1987 FX Softails

Both the basic Softail and the Softail Custom were back for 1987, with only minor updates. Late in the season, Harley-Davidson added a third Softail, the FXST-S Softail Special.

The Softail Special was a very limited edition of the basic Softail. It differed mainly in that it was given a special (and very handsome) two-tone paint scheme: Candy Brandywine with Brilliant Silver tank panels and silver and red pinstripes on both the tanks and fenders. Harley's figures show that only 398 were built.

The basic Softail was available in Vivid Black with red pinstripes, Candy Brandywine with red pinstripes, Candy Bronze with red pinstripes, and Metallic Blue with red and silver pinstripes. The Softail Custom was available in Vivid Black with silver pinstripes on both tanks and fenders, Candy Crimson with gold pinstripes on tanks and fenders, Candy Crimson with Candy Brandywine tank panels and red pinstripes on tanks and fenders, and Brilliant Candy Blue with Brilliant Silver tank panels and maroon and silver pinstripes on tanks and fenders. Frames were color-matched for all, but now in powdercoat rather than the paint used in 1986.

Once again, the Softails were the sales leaders of the Harley lineup. First among them was the Softail Custom (outselling the standard Softail almost three to one, and even outselling the 883 Sportster for the first time), followed by the Heritage Softail, standard Softail, Heritage Special, and Softail Special.

The FXSTS Springer Softail and the 1988 Updates

Great ideas always have one thing in common: they seem all too obvious in retrospect. The original FXST Softail of 1984 was one. The FLST Heritage Softail of 1986 was another. For model year 1988, Harley-Davidson introduced the third in what

Right: These tank transfers replaced the "winged ball" transfers used on 1985 Softails.

Below: From 1985 on, Softails carried a 120-mph speedometer, instead of the federally mandated 85-mph speedometer fitted for 1984.

would later become an even longer string of great ideas: the FXSTS Springer Softail, created by bolting up a modernized version of Harley's old springer front end. And, like all great ideas, it was seemingly simple in concept, but a great deal of work in the actual execution.

Recollections differ about who first voiced the idea. Many of those interviewed for this book say it was from Styling, but others said the idea came from within Engineering. Nevertheless, one thing is clear: within the company, the idea was immediately recognized for its greatness. Remembered Vaughn Beals: "I don't recall the genesis of the idea, but there was no discussion about do we want to do it or not. There was total unanimity that it made sense for the company. I loved the idea because it gave us a way to attract new customers and screw the Japanese because they didn't have anything like it in their heritage to go back to. The only problem was that making it happen took longer than any of us would like to have seen."

Team Springer

"We all knew that there were major problems with the old springer, with stiffness,

ride quality, and so forth," remembered then vice president of engineering Mark Tuttle, "so we put a group together to look at the feasibility." We'll call that group "Team Springer," an extension of the team (headed by Ron Hutchinson) that had worked its magic in getting the Softail to market so quickly.

Harley-Davidson's engineering standards for the updated springer front end were high: it had to work well, give adequate fork travel, allow for a disc brake, look like the old springer, and have modern durability. The team quickly began studying how to bring the old spring fork up to date.

The regular FXST Softail was also back for 1986, also with the new frame and five-speed transmission.

Above: Harley's five-speed transmission was designed for electric start only, so when the Softail got the five-speed for 1986, it lost its kickstarter.

Above right: The Softail's chopperesque 21-inch front laced wheel and bikini fender.

The first problem, according to team member Rit Booth, was that they didn't just have an old springer front end lying on the shelf. "We had to buy one from somebody that had old stuff," he remembered.

After studying the old parts, it was simple enough for the team engineers to employ their well-proven finite-element-analysis techniques to optimize the position of the pivots and the length of the links for better geometry, to increase its stiffness, and to increase wheel travel to a goal of 4 inches. Similarly straightforward were the tasks of designing the clever links that allow use of a modern disc brake and pivoting fender with the redesigned springer. (On the original springer, with about 2 inches of travel, the fender was fixed in place; the new springer was to have twice as much travel, so it was decided to make the fender move with the wheel to avoid the "motocross" look.)

Then they tested the updated springer built on the old fork, and ran up against a problem that stymied the whole effort for quite some time: how to get modern durability out of the bearings on the fork's rockers. "Remember," said then chief engineer Don Valentine, "the old rockers at the bottom of the forks had bushings and grease fittings. No matter what you did, those bushings would wear out and get sloppy real fast."

Harley-Davidson trumped its competitors by doing what only it had the heritage to do: bringing back an updated version of its old springer forks on the FXSTS Springer Softail.

So, that's where the team stalled for a while. "That was a very tough engineering process," recalled Vaughn Beals. "Jeff [Bleustein, then vice president of engineering] will tell you that I chewed his ass lots of times on that one because it seemed to me that it wasn't beyond our abilities to do it.

As was often the case, in our conservative approach, we would conclude that something wasn't practical, and the next thing you knew, you could go to a dealership and you could ride one. Somebody who hadn't been to MIT [that's as much a cut on himself as on anyone because Beals has a master's

degree in aeronautical engineering from MIT] would figure out how to do it. That put some pressure on."

Finally, engineer Tom McGowan found some reinforced Teflon-lined half-spherical bearings from a company named Aurora. "One day," recalled Rit Booth, "Tom said, 'Here's these things they use in aircraft. They gotta be pretty tough. Let's try 'em.' And they worked."

"The breakthrough was the half-spherical bearings," affirmed Mark Tuttle, "because they were adjustable and created so much more load surface. When Tom came up with those bearings, we went back to styling and said we had a concept that would allow us to do a modern springer."

(As an aside, one wonders whether the idea for using the half-spherical bearings came about as a result of Bill Davis' Sub Shock prototype, which used spherical Teflon bearings, a design feature carried over on the production Softails.)

After prototypes were built with the new bearings, testing proved that the new Springer was durable enough for the modern world, requiring adjustment at about 10,000-mile intervals. Better yet, it actually provided a more compliant ride than modern telescopic forks. And shock absorber

Above: Just like the original, the modern springer fork flaunted its mechanical bits, especially the two spring stacks flanking the center-mounted shock absorber.

Right: Like the Heritage Softail, the Softail Springer was fitted with the smaller version of the twin tanks. For 1988, Springers were numbered limited editions that celebrated Harley-Davidson's 85th anniversary. Only 1,450 were built.

Above: Springer front fenders carried this 85th-anniversary graphic.

technology had come a long way in the 40 years since the springer front suspension had been out of production, so the new dampers developed with shock manufacturer Monroe actually did a reasonable job of controlling the Springer's 21-inch wheel.

Just when the team thought the challenges were licked, new ones surfaced during pilot production. "It was a very significant manufacturing challenge," said Tuttle. "In the forgings and oval shapes on the legs, you'd get stress risers and cracking if you didn't do it right. We spent as much time solving the manufacturing problems as the engineering problems." In solving those problems, the Harley team

That's a profile no one thought they'd ever see on a new Harley again. Using computer modeling, Harley engineers modernized the old fork by optimizing the locations of the pivots, redesigning it for almost twice the travel of the old version, and devising linkages to allow use of a disc brake.

Springers were given the chrome-and-black engine of the Softail Custom.

Right: Even the gas caps were special on the 1988 Springer.

Below: Spare the chrome, spoil the Softail. Harley didn't spare the chrome on the Springer.

finally resorted to complex forgings and investment castings.

"It was a real bitch to make!" affirmed Tom Gelb, then vice president of operations. "With that mechanical setup, there were a million parts, and I mean they were all polished and chromed. It was a very labor-intensive process." All that chrome was subject to cracking on the more stressed parts of the fork, so Harley-Davidson was forced to use the more expensive triple plating process. "At the time," joked Gelb, "we were just hoping we wouldn't sell too many of them. I think at one time we told them we couldn't make more than 10 springer front ends a day."

Eventually, those problems were solved by farming out many of the castings and forgings to other companies, and the FXSTS Springer Softail made its debut midyear in the 1988 lineup to derisive snorts from the racer crowd and admiring whistles from just about everyone else. Even the mainstream motorcycling press loved it, commenting that the new fork was not only stiffer and more comfortable than the old telescopic unit (except over really harsh

The Softail Springer
was styled to look
like an older
chopper, not an
antique. Its 21-inch
front wheel and
bikini fender
established that
distinction.

bumps), but that it worked so well that it accentuated the weaknesses in the Softail rear suspension.

On top of all that function, Harley dished up high-test good looks, featuring the slimmer (4.2-gallon) Fat Bob tanks of the regular Softail, black paint with red and yellow pinstripes, the blacked-out and chromed engine from the Softail Custom, 85th-anniversary tank graphics, and all that chrome on the front end. Needless to say, the 1,300 numbered copies of this limited-edition classic sold out almost instantly, despite being priced at nearly $11,000, almost $1,400 more than for the regular Softail.

Softail and Softail Custom

The Softail and Softail Custom returned with many minor updates to the engine and

chassis. The most important of these updates was new forks featuring 39-mm tubes in place of the willowy 35-mm units previously used.

Once again, though sales for the U.S. motorcycle industry were down by about 28 percent, Harley's sales reached new heights, up nearly 14 percent. The Softail models were responsible for most of the increase.

The 1989 FX Softails

Both the Softail and the Custom were back for 1989, with few changes. Styling was modernized by new primary cases that hid the starter, and the ride was improved by new shocks with adjustable preload for the springs and a very welcome 1/2 inch more travel.

Right: In 1993, the front fender and its linkage to the fork were revised to lower the fender closer to the tire to reduce the dreaded "motocross" look shown on this 1991 machine.

Opposite: Harley-Davidson gave the Springer a laced rear wheel, rather than the Softail Custom's disc wheel.

Once again, Softail sales were up substantially, despite the fact that the whole motorcycle market in the United States was still contracting and the Softails were some of the most expensive bikes in the Harley line. Even more surprising, the more expensive Custom and Classic versions outsold the plain ones by three- or four-to-one margins. Naturally, profits soared. Still sales king of the whole Harley line was the Softy Custom. Sales of the plain-Jane Softail fell way behind. The lesson illustrated is one Harley-Davidson has taken to heart: blacked-out engines and more chrome result in higher sales, despite the higher prices.

For 1995, Harley-Davidson released a custom version of the Springer, the FXSTB Bad Boy, with gloss black replacing much of the chrome.

Bad Boy forks were black, highlighted by chrome springs and shocks.

The 1990 FX Softails

For 1990, the Softail tanks were given new "eagle's head" transfers, and the engines were fitted with constant-velocity (CV) carbs and a revised clutch.

Yet again, the Softail Custom was the best-selling bike in Harley's lineup. Sales of the plain FXST trailed so badly that it was discontinued at the end of the model year. By this time, Harley was selling every bike it could build, so it made sense to discontinue the lower-priced FXST, leaving that much more of its production capacity for building premium-priced Customs.

The 1991 Softail Custom

Softail Custom was the only regular-fork FX Softail model for 1991, and it returned with only minor changes to the engine and cosmetics for the new year. Fortunately, sales didn't suffer for all this lack of improvement. The Softail Custom did lose its place as Harley's sales leader, however. The Heritage Softail Classic outsold the Custom, 8,950 to 7,525.

The 1992 Softail Custom

Softail Custom was again the sole regular FX Softail model. Its engine was updated with a Dyna-style oiling system and revised jetting in the carb to improve cold-starting. Its look was updated with new tank emblems that featured a star being dive-bombed by an eagle, talons brandished, re-creating the look of the U.S. Army Air Force's unit insignia of World War II.

Harley also improved the Softail Custom (and all the others, too) with a new process that made the paint more durable. Harley had long (and justifiably) been famous for the quality of its paintwork. But the quality of that paint reached whole new heights in 1992, when the company turned the key on its new paint facility, which gave the company the capability to do what many had tried but few had actually pulled off: apply a powder clear coat as smooth and glossy as the best sprayed-on paint.

Powdercoat is really tough stuff—far more resistant to chipping than normal sprayed-on paints. If you've ever looked at the powdercoating most places apply, however, you'll see that it looks pretty smooth—until you get close. Certainly, it's good enough for frames and some brackets (which Harley does powdercoat), but not

Above: Bad Boy brakes. Harley fitted FXSTBs with floating brake rotors.

Left: Bad Boys featured a unique slotted aluminum rear wheel and floating rear rotors.

Bad Boy was a custom Springer for the 1990s.

good enough for the tanks and fenders of $10,000 motorcycles. With help from its suppliers, Harley developed a process good enough to fool the most discerning eye. In the new process, a two-step corrosion-control coating is applied, followed by sprayed-on base and color coats, followed by the powder clear and a trip through the oven. The result is the best-looking and toughest paint in the industry.

Left: Bad Boy's engine was the chrome-and-black beauty used in all the other custom models, topped off by its own unique air-cleaner cover.

Below: The basic theme was black, with a few well-chosen chrome highlights.

The 1993–98 Softail Customs

Softail Custom was back for Harley's 90th-anniversary year with few changes. Oddly, none of the Softails were offered in the special 90th-anniversary trim that was offered on many of the other lines. The most important updates for the year were higher gearing to lower engine rpm at cruise and new "low-profile" brake and clutch levers.

There were no notable changes for 1994. For 1995, the Softail Custom was given a minor restyle courtesy of new tank transfers that featured "Harley-Davidson" over a diamond shape superimposed over a stylized eagle in flight. For 1996, the Softail Custom got a new, electronically driven speedometer. Harley changed little on the Custom for 1997. For 1998 it was given a new clutch that had been reworked for lower lever effort to disengage it.

Night Train, Softail Standard, and the 1999 Softail Custom

Harley-Davidson kick-started a "new iron age" for the company in 1999 with the release of the thumping new Twin Cam 88 motor. This engine was basically new from top to bottom (Harley-Davidson says only 21 functional parts are shared between it

Bad Boys were built from 1995 to 1997. Shown is a 1997 model.

and the Evo engine). Harley put its new engine in all the Big Twins—except the Softails.

After eight years as the only regular-fork FX Softail, the Custom got two new siblings for 1999: the FXSTB Night Train and the FXST Softail Standard. All were still powered by the trusty Evolution engine.

The FXSTB Night Train
The original FXSTB had been the black-on-black Springer-based Bad Boy of 1995–97 (see chapter 4). For 1999, Willie and Louie put a new blacked-out "bad boy" in the lineup, the FXSTB Night Train. It was based on the Softail Custom, using that model's

Harley-Davidson released a new Softail for 1999 that took the blacked-out theme of the discontinued Bad Boy to the next extreme. That bike was the FXSTB Night Train. Night Train was based on the Softail Custom, with a disc rear wheel and the larger, 5-gallon Fat Bob tanks, but the theme here was flat black.

conventional forks, 5.2-gallon tanks, and disc rear wheel.

Even blacker than the Bad Boy had been, the Night Train wasn't just black, it was matte black, like a Stealth Fighter, with black crinkle on the oil tank, the entire engine (except the pushrod tubes and fasteners), the tranny cases and covers, and the rear fender supports. Just about everything else was shiny black, save the fork assembly. Its tanks were fitted with a unique diamond emblem.

Lean, ever so black, and with a performance edge courtesy of the 6-inch straight

The Night Train got its own engine, set apart from all the others by almost complete coverage of wrinkle black. Even the rocker boxes were coated black, and the fin ends weren't polished, either.

On the Night Train, even the primary cases were wrinkle black. If you're fed up with the "chrome-everything" movement, here's a bike for you.

(no pullback) chrome risers topped with flat drag bars, the Night Train was probably the best-looking blacked-out Harley yet, proving that juicy styling treats could still be wrung out of the old Evo Softail.

The FXST Softail Standard

Making a surprise reprise was a new version of the plain old FXST (which had been axed at the end of 1990), now officially dubbed the Softail Standard.

With so many versions of the Softail already available, and waiting lists for every one built, why would Harley-Davidson backtrack and reintroduce a plain-Jane Softail? I think it all comes down to another Willie-and-Louie counter-chrome styling statement. If the Night Train was the "Stealth Softail," the Standard was "Subtle Softail," with the matte silver of its engine castings glowing softly against the Vivid Black paint.

For 1999, only the Softail models and two special-edition FXR models were fitted with the Evolution engine. For 2000, the Evolution would be gone even on the Softails, replaced by the Twin Cam 88B engine, with twin counterbalancers. And the Softail Custom was dropped, leaving the Night Train as the custom Softail for the start of the Twin Cam era.

Here's where we see how much had changed in the decade and a half that the Softail was in production. In 1984, the "plain" Softail was the swankest, most "custom" bike in the whole Harley lineup—in any company's lineup, for that matter. Just 15 model years later, the original Softail would look as much of a stripper compared to the '99 Softails as the 883 Sportster does compared to the Sportster 1200 Custom. Well, the Softail Standard was even less flashy than the original Softail, showing how far Willie and Louie pushed it to make their statement.

The dynamic duo took back all the extras that had been added in 1986 to create the Softail Custom—disc wheel, blacked and polished engine and tranny, sissy bar, and so on. But they went even further, replacing the chrome on the oil tank with gloss black and foregoing even the polish on the primary cover. In fact, except for the polish on the rocker covers, the whole motor wore its satin silver finish as a proud mark of distinction. Though the masses clearly preferred the blacked-out and polished motor of the other Softails, for a certain group, the plain-silver motor of the Standard really scratched an itch—and left

a few bucks in their pockets that they could spend on the custom touches that mattered most to them.

The Softail Custom was back with little change, except for one part restyled like that of the new Twin Cam 88: a gleaming new derby cover with five mounting screws (instead of three).

End of an Era

At the end of the 1999 model year, the Evolution motor was discontinued and a wildly successful era ended for Harley-Davidson and for the Softails. When both began, the company was one overadvance away from bankruptcy and Harley's motorcycles were derided as unreliable, overpriced, and hopelessly outdated relics of the bad old days of motorcycling. By the end of 1999, the Motor Company was the most profitable motorcycle manufacturer in the world and its motorcycles were mainstream objects of desire.

Fortunately, an exciting new era for both the Softail and the Motor Company was about to begin. We'll pick up with that story in chapter 4. First, let's take a closer look at a special slice of the Softail line.

THREE

THE HERITAGE SPECIALS, 1986–1999

"Once we had the Softail, we could do all kinds of wondrous things with it."

—Vaughn Beals, former CEO of Harley-Davidson

Choppers are not for everyone. They're not very versatile, for one, and some guys don't like the look. Actually, it's not so much that they didn't like the look, it's more that they just loved the looks of those classic '50s Hydra-Glides more than the looks of one that had been chopped. We'll call them the Hydra-Gliders.

Success of the Softail proved that the chopper boys were willing to pay big bucks for a turnkey chop with modern comfort and convenience. Wouldn't Hydra-Gliders be willing to do the same to get a bike that looked like a vintage FLH but ran like a modern Harley?

That was the question Harley-Davidson sought to answer with the midyear introduction of the retro-styled Heritage Softail in 1986. In building the Heritage, Harley unchopped the Softail. In doing so, the Harley design team revived the simple, bold lines of the old FL Hydra-Glide hardtails made from 1949 to 1957.

All the really important styling cues were there, in all the places that old Bill Harley had originally put them. The "fat" front look was courtesy of the shrouded fork, valanced front fender, and 16-inch front wheel, just as in 1949. For the top shroud of that fork, Willie G. revived the more stylish design first seen in 1955, with three chevrons standing proud on each side of the gleaming chrome headlight. Fattening up the rear was a version of the old FLH valanced rear fender. Also blasting back from the past to help complete the '50s look were a bunch of other updated parts, including the slimmer, 3.5-gallon version of the Fat Bob saddle tanks used on all the Knuckles and Pans prior to the Electra Glide of 1965 (and on some afterward)—rather than the 5-gallon tanks of the regular Softails—wide buckhorn bars, and footboards. Signal Red paint with Cream tank panels, highlighted by pinstriping, carried through the illusion of age. The

Opposite: Midway through the 1986 model year, Harley-Davidson introduced this machine, the FLST Heritage Softail. The new Heritage brought back the look of the Hydra-Glides of the mid-1950s.

While most of the rest of the Heritage was plain old Softail, the front end was a special new piece, designed to recapture the look of the fat front end of the old Hydra-Glides. For the styling on the headlight and fork shrouds, Willie G. Davidson reprised the three-chevron design first used from 1955 to 1959.

me the extra cush would be a waste on any Softail. Alas, it was not to be, as modern tastes demanded low seat heights, at the expense of comfort.

These quibbles from an old-Harley geek aside, the Heritage was another masterpiece from the styling department, and one that got noticed everywhere, most notably on the sales floor. *Cycle* called it a "machine of arresting simplicity" and "the most elegant Harley-Davidson of its generation." To their delight, those who bought the new Heritage soaked up the compliments when passersby exclaimed, "Nice old Hog!" and grinned when asked, "What year is it?" Satisfying, indeed, the Heritage found a soft spot in nearly everyone.

Riding Backwards

Getting that look required far more than just a raid on the obsolete parts bin, however. "The biggest challenge was that we were going backwards from a low-inertia front end to a high-inertia front end," said Mark Tuttle, then vice president of engineering. He continued, "The biggest issues were getting the high-speed stability and handling right. We put a fair amount of effort into making that combination of frame and front end functional."

Initially, Harley engineers put an old-style front end on the Softail to see how it would do. The results weren't encouraging: "It went around corners kind of like an old FL," remembered Rit Booth (who was then product manager for the FX line), "and that wasn't good enough anymore."

From all the earlier work done on refining the FLHT's handling (read all about it in the book *Harley-Davidson Evolution Motorcycles*, also published by MBI), Harley's engineers knew that the key to improving the handling of the Heritage Softail front end was to center as much of the mass as

rest was pure Softail—chrome horseshoe oil tank, rigid-rear look, five-speed tranny, and so on.

Add a tractor seat and replace the shorty duals with the proper '50s two-into-one and you'd fool even the old-Harley mavens—from a distance, anyway. Hey, the frame tube to mount the seat post was still there, so why not? You can't tell

In the 1950s, the Hydra-Glides had the 3.5-gallon twin tanks, so that's what the Heritage was given, even though the other Softails for 1986 had the wider 5-gallon tanks.

A fat 16-inch front wheel and skirted fender were important parts of the Hydra-Glide look, too, as was the two-tone paint on the tank. This 1986 Heritage sports its original paint, Signal Red and Cream.

close as possible to the steering axis. To get it right, Booth and company reengineered every part, lightening everything possible, paying special attention to the heavy fender. To lighten the front and rear of the fender (the parts farthest from the steering axis), Booth and company designed a lighter front fender tip and bobbed the rear of the fender, replacing a big chunk of steel with a lighter aluminum trim strip. Side-to-side

mass was tucked in closer by decreasing the spacing between the fork legs as much as Styling would allow.

All that work to refine the handling forced changes to the triple clamps, so while Booth and company were at that, they took the opportunity to redesign the clamps to allow even more 1950s character: "The last version of the FL had this cast aluminum housing for the headlight. Its

A teardrop-shaped toolbox wasn't standard on the first Heritage, but it certainly looks like it belongs. This view shows how well hidden the rear suspension really is on the Softails. Soon, the Heritage spawned its own line. First came the Heritage Special in 1987, with the chrome-and-black engine, special seat, and leather saddlebags. The Special became the Heritage Custom in 1988.

triple clamps wouldn't work for the Heritage project, so we decided to go way back to a stand-alone bullet headlight and two-piece stamping that went around the triple clamp. I was working with Bill [Willie G.] Davidson at the time, so I went back to him. Turns out that older look was really what he wanted anyway, but everyone had said that that would be the hard way to go. Turned out it was the easiest way to go." That older look, with the stand-alone headlight, had been a signature feature of all the Hydra-Glides and of the Duo-Glides of 1958 and 1959.

To help get the overall look even more right—"We wanted the lower frame rails horizontal, like on the old FLs, not sloping uphill toward the front like on the regular Softail," Booth explained—the engineers used fork tubes about an inch and a half longer than those on the old Hydra-Glide front end.

So, how did it all work? Perfectly for the Heritage's target audience. Though the Heritage had the look of the classic 1950s touring bikes, Harley knew that few Heritages would actually be turned into baggers. This machine was all about looks,

Softail enthusiast Jerry Sanden on the first-year Heritage he has owned since it was new. He also bought a Softail in 1984 and later bought a Springer.

and those looks came with compromises. The Heritage was a great ride, so long as you didn't wick it up too much (the vibration at 85 mph is not bearable for long), tilt the horizon too far (unless you love the sound of footboards scraping across asphalt), or stay in the saddle too long (unless you love that tingling feeling in your fingers). But for oozing along at 60 to 70 for a few hours or for a night on the town, it was 650 pounds of rolling grace.

In its ads, the company called it "a legacy fulfilled." Truly, it was, and the Heritage was a resounding success in its first year. All 2,510 sold as fast as they could be built. Like the original Softail before it, the Heritage went on to spawn its own distinct model line—and its own imi-

tators, for Willie G.'s shadow disciples in Japan were watching.

The 1987 Heritage Softails

For 1987, the Heritage was joined by a new special-edition sibling, the FLST-S Heritage Softail Special. Tanks on both Heritage models were uprated to 4.2 gallons (from 3.5 gallons). Little else was changed, except for the color options.

Echoing the theme from the Softail Custom of the year before, Harley's new Heritage Special was the basic package with a bunch of additions that accentuated the true character of the machine. With a blacked-out and polished engine, more chrome, custom two-tone paint on tanks and fenders, a Lexan windshield, passing

lamps, leather saddlebags, and a special two-piece seat and backrest with studs and conchos, the Special was the soul of the 1950s tourer and was offered in only one color combination: Metallic Blue with Cream tank and fender panels and red and gold pinstripes.

The 1988 and 1989 Heritage Softails

The FLST Heritage Softail was back for 1988, along with a new "baggerized" version of the Heritage, the FLSTC Heritage Softail Classic. The Classic package included a chrome-and-black treatment on the engine, a touring windshield, dual chrome passing lamps, and a leather seat and backrest and leather saddlebags, all with stud-and-concho trim.

For 1989, the Heritage and Heritage Classic returned with a few notable updates. The shocks on all the Softails were redesigned to offer adjustable preload for the springs and a very welcome 3/4-inch-more travel. For even more of a '50s touring look, the Heritage Classic got fishtail muffler tips.

For 1990, Harley-Davidson dropped a new bomb on the motorcycling world, the FLSTF Fat Boy. Its silver and rivet styling was reminiscent of the B-29 Superfortresses of World War II.

Fat Boy's most notable new feature was its aluminum disc front and rear wheels.

Overall, the U.S. motorcycle market continued its decade-long death spin in 1989, as new-bike sales fell a further 28 percent. That year, the overall market for streetbikes was *one-third* the size it had been in 1981. Despite that, Harley-Davidson's sales rose 17 percent, to 55,507, the first time the company had topped 50,000 since 1976, and even more impressive when you consider that back in 1976, many of those sales were of the Aermacchi two-strokes, whereas in 1989 they were all Sportsters and Big Twins. Once again, Harley took the lead in sales of over-850-cc motorcycles, with 46.5 percent of the mar-

ket. Another new trend: sales figures were starting to reflect Harley-Davidson's production capacity more than the actual demand. Waiting lists began for the most popular models. The Heritage Classic was among them.

Fat Boy and the 1990 Heritage Models

With the Heritage and Heritage Classic, Harley took its Softail back to the 1950s. For the start of the new decade, the company unveiled a new version of the Heritage that updated the look into the 1990s. Harley's bold new Heritage was named the

Left: Fat Boy introduced a new style of exhaust, the over-under shotgun design.

Below: Frame and oil tank were also painted silver and set off by yellow highlights, as shown here on the derby cover and rocker covers.

FLSTF Fat Boy, and it was a production replica of the custom Heritage ridden to Daytona by Willie G. in 1988.

Fat Boy featured a futuristic industrial look, courtesy of its sleek Fine Silver Metallic paint slathered onto not only the gas tanks and fenders, but also the frame, swingarm, oil tank, fork sliders, and fender supports. Fat rubber framed solid disk wheels. As the Harley ads for it pointed out, Fat Boy was "sweating with custom details."

Highlighting the silver monochrome look were yellow "hot spots" on the center rocker-box spacers, on the customized timing cover on the right and "derby" clutch cover on the left, on the tank console, and on the all-new Fat Boy tank emblem. A big part of Fat Boy's look was the new over-under shotgun-style dual exhaust that made Fat Boy look even longer and lower. The turn signals were moved to the fender supports and the tip light on the rear fender was left off to give a cleaner look to the rear. The front fender was bobbed and flared at the rear and stripped of lights and trim. Completing the silver-on-silver look were

Harley's model brochure called the Fat Boy a "heavy-duty hunk of style" and pointed out that it was "sweating" with custom details— dozens of unique parts that gave it a distinctly different look from the Heritage.

twin 16-inch disc wheels with polished rims and rough-cast centers and an un-painted engine.

Fat Boy exuded industrial chic. It had the tough look of bolts and rivets and plate steel. In fact, the only parts soft and hu-manistic about it were the pigskin seat with hand-laced detailing on the seat valance and the hand-laced leather tank trim. It was, as the ad said, "a heavy-duty hunk of style," but if the Heritage was a rolling Elvis tune, Fat Boy was Nine Inch Nails forced to play in the triplet cadence of a Harley V-twin. As the ad so aptly continued, "This Harley doesn't invite comment, it demands

it." Fat Boy was also the natural choice as Arnold Schwartzenegger's ride in the movie *Terminator 2*, filmed the next year.

The other Heritage models were back, with a few changes. Engines in both were fit-ted with a stronger clutch, new starter, and larger carburetor. Heritage Classic models got redesigned leather bags with new mounts that made doffing the bags easier.

For 1990, the Softail Custom and Heritage Classic were numbers 1 and 2 in sales, at 6,795 and 5,483 (respectively), trouncing even the cheap 883 Sportster. Coming in at number 4 was the Fat Boy on the block, with 4,440 sold. Sales of the

Fat Boy's silver-on-silver look was used only for 1990. In the following years, it was available in any color an owner wanted.

Fat Boy's bobbed front fender hugged the tire like the wheel pants on a 1920s biplane.

plain Heritage fell to 1,567, so it was dropped from the lineup at the end of the year. Waiting lists lengthened, and profits soared.

The 1991 Heritage Models
The year 1991 brought a lot of change to the Harley lineup, most notably the intro-

duction of the five-speed Sportster and the all-new Dyna Sturgis, and the elimination of the standard versions of the Softail and Heritage Softail. Heritage Classic and Fat Boy were back with a few internal engine changes.

Fat Boy also lost his silver-on-silver industrial look and yellow "hot spots," in favor

Fat Boy's unique tank badges look like they were inspired by U.S. Army Air Forces unit emblems of World War II.

Fat Boy was also given a unique leather seat and pony express–sized saddlebags.

Silver, rivets, and
yellow highlights.
Who can deny the
family resemblance?

Harley's most moo-
velous new model for
1993 was the FLSTN
Heritage Nostalgia.

of bright new color combinations, a blacked-out engine, and a lot more chrome. With all those changes, Fat Boy took on a new character. It was a Heritage that didn't look old. Nevertheless, it still looked like a classic. Some say it's the best-looking Harley since the first Knucklehead of 1936.

The Heritage Classic was the best-selling Harley for the first time. Harley-Davidson sold 8,950 Classics, relegating the Softail

Nostalgia was a Heritage with a few Fat Boy touches. Shown here are the Fat Boy–type seat and tank emblems.

Custom to number 2, with 7,525 sales. In number 3 was another surprise, the XLH-1200 Sportster, beating out the cheaper XL-883, which was number 5. The bright new Fat Boy came in number 4, with 5,581 sales.

The 1992 Heritage Models

The Heritage Classic and Fat Boy were back for 1992, with a few functional changes such as the revised oil system from the Dyna, and revised jetting in the carb to improve cold-starting. New paint options were available for all. And, like all the Harleys that year, the paint was made extradurable by the new powder clear coat.

Heritage Nostalgia and the 1993 Updates

The year 1993 was Harley-Davidson's 90th-anniversary season and the Motor Company celebrated with the introduction of a new cut on the Softail chassis, the FLSTN Heritage Softail Nostalgia. It was the only Softail model given a special treatment for the anniversary.

To create the Nostalgia, Willie G. and Louie N. blended the styling of the Heritage Classic, the Fat Boy, and the Softail Custom, and they also gave it a few parts of its own that added to its "moo-ving" good looks. Starting with the Classic, they added the Fat

Left: Nineteen ninety-three was Harley-Davidson's 90th anniversary, and the company celebrated by releasing the Nostalgia as a numbered limited edition. Only 2,700 were built. Tanks on the Nostalgia were the larger, 5.2-gallon type from the Softail Custom.

Below: The only color scheme offered was Birch White with Vivid Black panels on both tanks and fenders, with red and gray pinstriping. Harley-Davidson's 1993 model brochure asked of the Heritage, "Who would have thought black and white could be so colorful?"

Boy's shotgun exhaust, leather seat, wide FLH bars, tank emblem, and leather tank trim, but with a few important differences: fishtail mufflers replaced Fat Boy's straight ones, the tank emblems were chrome and fired enamel, and hair-on, black-and-white Holstein hide was stitched in place of the textured inserts on the seat. From the Softail Custom came the 5-gallon über–Fat Bob tanks. New to the line were the "fat gangster whitewalls" on the laced wheels and the pony express–sized Fat Boy saddlebags, also with Holstein inserts. Paintwork carried through the Holstein theme— Birch White with Vivid Black panels on both tanks and fenders, with red and gray pinstriping.

Nostalgic it was, but, like the Fat Boy, it was a modern custom expression of a classic look, and it didn't look old. Said Harley of the new machine, "Who would have thought black and white could be so colorful?"

As a result of flaunting so much hair-on cowhide, the Nostalgia soon was tagged with several appropriate nicknames: Moo Glide, Cow Glide, or Heritage Holstein, depending on who's talking. And, naturally enough, all 2,700 numbered copies sold out quicker than you can tip a cow.

Above: Black-and-white hair-on cowhide inserts on the seat inspired several nicknames for the 1993 Nostalgia, among them Moo Glide, Cow Glide, and Heritage Holstein.

Left: The Nostalgia's tank badges are styled like the Fat Boy's, but on the Nostalgia they're metal, rather than stickers.

The bull horns shown here are not an official Harley-Davidson accessory, though they look natural on the Cow Glide.

Both the Heritage Classic and Fat Boy were back for 1993, with a few minor updates that were added to the whole Softail line: higher gearing to lower engine rpm at cruise and new "low-profile" brake and clutch levers.

The 1994–96 Heritage Models

For 1994, the Heritage Classic and Fat Boy were back with only minor updates. The FLSTN was back, too, with the same updates, plus a few of its own. Harley-Davidson called it the Heritage Softail

Special, instead of Nostalgia. If it was "Special" instead of "Nostalgia," why didn't Harley change its alpha designation to "FLSTS"? Probably because the Motor Company was saving that serving of alphabet soup for 1997. The Special retained the hairy inserts on the seat and saddlebags, but for 1994 they were all black, rather than black and white.

Right: The Cow Glide came with Fat Boy–style saddlebags, but these were also given Holstein inserts.

Below: A Fat Boy–style over-under shotgun exhaust with fishtail mufflers was unique to the Nostalgia.

The Special's stunning paint scheme of Birch White with silver panels, set off by red and gray pinstriping, was its most striking new feature. Put simply, it was pretty—perhaps too pretty for the average biker. Harley knew it, too. Said Harley of its new beauty: "If we ever design a motorcycle everyone likes, we've failed. The Softail Special is a prime example of that. . . . Either you get it or you don't."

Fat Boy, Heritage Classic, and Heritage Special were all offered again in 1995. The Special got yet another paint scheme change, though. This time it was to Charcoal Satinbrite with Vivid Black panels on the tank and fenders. Seats and saddlebags were

Left: "Fat gangster whitewalls" on laced wheels complemented the Holstein theme.

Above: Also from the Fat Boy were the wider, FLH-style bars.

Right: Holstein detailing extended to the backrest.

For 1994, the FLSTN
was back, but Harley-
Davidson called it the
Heritage Special
instead of Nostalgia.

Harley-Davidson is known for the excellence of its color combinations. Still, some consider the 1994 Special's white and silver to be the best of the 1990s.

Right: Heritage Special's Birch White paint with silver panels, set off by red and gray pinstriping, was its most striking new feature.

Below: All the Holstein was gone, but a bit of the cow still remained. Black hair-on inserts still graced the seat and backrest.

trimmed with chromed bullet studs, and the hairy inserts were replaced by panels of charcoal leather.

For 1996, all three Heritage models returned, with electronic speedometers, and the Special's styling was revised again. Painted Mystique Green with Platinum Silver panels, the 1996 Special also sported restyled Fat Boy tank emblems and regular Fat Boy bags and seat, with black panels replacing the gray ones of 1995. The Special was discontinued at the end of the model year.

Heritage Springer and the 1997 Updates

What to do after successfully reviving the looks of the classic '50 Hydra-Glides? Why not revive the looks of the even-more-classic springer Knuckleheads and Panheads of the 1930s and 1940s? That's what Harley-Davidson did for 1997 when it released a new model with styling that could stop time: the FLSTS Heritage Softail Springer.

Willie G. and Louie N. did most of their work on the front, modifying the modernized spring fork from the Springer

Left: Saddlebags also flaunted the hair-on inserts.

Below: The Heritage Special was back for 1995 and 1996, with a unique paint scheme each year, but the model was canceled at the end of 1996.

For 1997, Harley-Davidson released another model with looks that could stop time—the FLSTS Heritage Springer.

Softail to fit a fat 16-inch front wheel and a chrome horn just as on the originals. Then they revived and updated the old springer front fender (but they mounted this one so it swings upward with the tire, unlike those of the 1940s) and its running lamp.

In the middle they bolted on a big saddle with outsized tooled-leather skirts, long leather fringe, red trim, chromed grab rail, and removable passenger section. A chromed crossover dual exhaust with fishtail mufflers swept back underneath fringed, tooled-leather bags. Then Willie and Louie carried the retro look all the way to the back by fitting the classic tombstone taillight first used on the 1947 Knuckle. For

Harley-Davidson wanted this Springer to look old, not like a chopper, so it was fitted with a fat 16-inch front wheel and larger fender. As on the regular Springer, just about every piece on the springer front end is polished and chromed.

the paint, they offered the Heritage Springer only in Birch White, with tank striping in blue or red, in the style first used on the 1936 flathead models. The chrome-plated cherry on the whole sundae was the tank emblem, which mimicked those on the 1940–47 Knuckles.

The Heritage Springer was an almost spot-on re-creation of the pimped-up bikes the bobber guys of the 1940s and

The Heritage Classic—once the most upscale Harley of them all—was the basic Heritage model in the 1990s. Shown is a 1995 model.

Left: The Heritage Classic was the best-selling Harley for most of the 1990s.

Below: Befitting its 1950s Hydra-Glide looks, the Heritage was fitted with footboards for the rider.

1950s derided as "garbage wagons." The truth is, all it needed to get rid of the "almost" was a tank-shift, the old post-mounted tractor seat, half-moon footboards, and a front fender mounted to the rigid leg of the fork and showing more of the tire, but we won't go there. After all, even Harley has to make concessions to modern tastes. Nevertheless, with a wink, the Harley-Davidson sales catalog unofficially dubbed it the "Ol' Boy."

As with the regular Springer Softail, the old look came at very little price in function.

Above: Harley-Davidson celebrated its 95th anniversary in 1998 by releasing several of the Heritage Springer and Fat Boy models in Anniversary trim.

Right: Each Anniversary model was numbered and decked out with unique Anniversary trim.

The spring fork is stiction-free, and its 4 inches of travel will absorb a hefty jolt before bottoming hard. For those who like to tilt the horizon, though, this isn't the bike. Just as with the regular Heritage, the Springer version grounds its footboards and other bits with gusto just when things are *starting* to get fun. No matter, though. Ridden as it was intended to be, it's quite possibly the most satisfying Big Twin in the Harley line.

Heritage Classic and Fat Boy were both back for 1997, with minor updates.

Anniversary Edition Heritage Models
The year 1998 was Harley-Davidson's 95th anniversary, and the company celebrated by releasing anniversary editions of the Fat Boy and Heritage Springer. These featured a special Midnight Red and Champagne Pearl paint job and a new fired-enamel cloisonné emblem commemorating the anniversary.

Heritage Classic was back, too, but wasn't offered in Anniversary trim. Non-anniversary Heritage Springers were painted Vivid Black with blue or red trim for 1998. All the Heritage models were updated with a new clutch that had been reworked for lower lever effort to disengage it.

1999 Heritage Models
Harley-Davidson kick-started a "new iron age" in 1999 with the release of the thumping new Twin Cam 88 motor. This engine was basically new from top to bottom. Harley put its new engine in all the Big Twins, except the Softails.

Fat Boy, Heritage Springer, and Heritage Classic were all back, put powered by the trusty old Evolution engine. They did get one part off the Twin Cam, however: a gleaming new derby cover with five mounting screws (instead of three).

Upper left: A Midnight Red and Champagne Pearl paint job and a new fired-enamel cloisonné emblem helped distinguish Anniversary models from all others.

Left: Heritage Springer's Anniversary trim included this embroidered emblem on the backrest.

Three thousand Anniversary Heritage Springers were built for 1998.

End of an Era

At the end of the year, the Evolution motor was discontinued and an era ended for Harley-Davidson and for the Heritage Softails. Fortunately, an exciting new era for both was about to begin.

FOUR

THE TWIN CAM SOFTAILS, 2000–2003

"It's the prettiest Softail custom we've ever announced."

—Vice president of styling Willie G. Davidson,

of his latest styling masterpiece, the Deuce

Times had changed greatly since 1984, when the first Softail thundered out of the gates at York, Pennsylvania, but the Softail had not.

In 1984, the Softail had no competition. It was hands down the most stylish factory bike on the planet. It was even more stylish than many one-off customs. The Japanese had just begun serious attempts at mimicking Harley style, and their efforts to that time were hideously inept. With the Softail Custom of 1986, Harley widened the lead and did it again and again with the Springer, Fat Boy, Bad Boy, and others.

By the late 1990s, however, others were catching up. With each successive year, Honda, Kawasaki, Suzuki, and Yamaha got closer to capturing the look and feel of the Softail and other Harleys. Polaris and Excelsior-Henderson fired up with new cruisers to try and sneak a piece of Harley's pie. And a biker's dozen of small manufacturers began building Harley-style bikes

from trick custom parts and aftermarket clones of the Evolution engine. Even the more radical Softails like the Bad Boy began to look plain as a nun next to the tarted-up clones. Harley-Davidson still had waiting lists for every bike it could build, so it was far from being in jeopardy. Nevertheless, looking to secure its future, the Motor Company quietly went to work on ideas to trump all challengers.

Fortunately, many things had also changed for the better, and those things gave Harley the resources to act decisively: First, Harley-Davidson was no longer on the brink of bankruptcy. Although it increased production every year, demand exceeded supply, even though retail prices went up every year. Add to this the amazing profits generated by its Parts and Accessories and MotorClothes divisions, and by the mid-1990s, Harley-Davidson was an economic powerhouse. Second, Engineering had grown from a mere

Opposite: Harley-Davidson released the second-generation Softails for 2000, all powered by the new Twin Cam 88B engine. Flagship of the second-generation line was the FXSTD Deuce, shown here.

Right: Most notably new on the Deuce was its stretched gas tank, which was unique to the model.

Below: Another Deuce-only feature was its deep-dish disc rear wheel. It carries a fat low-profile 160/70-17 tire.

handful of degreed engineers that were hard-pressed to work on more than one project at a time to a huge department that was the equal of any in the world in skill and experience.

Harley's response to all these challenges would be a "one-two" punch, in the words of former vice president of engineering Mark Tuttle, that would send the Japanese and Polaris reeling for the ropes and put the clone makers down for the count. Those two body blows were code-named P-22 "Alpha" and "Beta."

That first blow fell in model year 1999 when the new Twin Cam 88 engine (the P-22 Alpha project) was released in Harley's rubber-mounted Big Twins. On the outside the new engine didn't look all that different from the Evo, but it was almost entirely new on the inside, with a one-piece crankshaft, twin chain-driven camshafts, an entirely new oiling system, more displacement and power, and plenty of built-in room to grow in displacement and power.

The old Evo was essentially an update of the 1930s Knucklehead engine. All the important patents had long since expired, so anyone was free to build clones of it without any fear of lawsuits. Much of the Twin Cam

Left: The ruler-straight lower line of the Deuce's rear fender stretches back to cut the top curve of the fender. A recessed taillight keeps the look as streamlined as the aft end of a bullet train.

Below: Atop the stretched tank was a new chrome dash that updated the classic old piece for the new millennium.

was new and protected from aftermarket exploitation long into the future. And Harley further protected itself by designing the Twin Cam motor to put out more horsepower than the engines of most of the competition and by having its own hot-rodding parts available for the Twin Cam from day one. With these parts a buyer could pump up his new Harley engine with genuine factory parts and not void the warranty. With service like that from Milwaukee, who needed the aftermarket?

Harley's second blow crunched home for model year 2000, when it released a second version of the Twin Cam motor, the Twin Cam 88B (the P-22 Beta project), which it fitted to a whole line of reengineered Softails. The "B" stood for the counterbalancers built into the engine to take the peaks off the vibrations from the Softail's solidly mounted engine. That engine wasn't the whole story, however. From front to back, the Softails were reengineered to be trick enough and comfortable enough to give the Softail a commanding edge over its competitors for years to come.

The Y2K Twin Cam Softail line included most of the old favorites from the Evo era: FXST Softail Standard, FXSTB

Night Train, FXSTS Springer, FLSTC Heritage Classic, FLSTS Heritage Springer, and FLSTF Fat Boy. One was missing, however: the FXSTC Softail Custom, which was replaced for the Twin Cam era with a new custom Softail. We'll get back to that soon enough. But now let's look at what changed across the line.

Good Vibrations

Harley engines vibrate; everyone knows that. Those vibes are a natural consequence of the 45-degree angle between the cylinders that gives the motor its great looks. Fortunately, though, Harley vibes are good ones. In small doses they are evidence of soul in the machine, a beating heart that makes riding a Harley feel like riding a living beast. On the solid-mounted Softails, however, those vibes are piped through uncut from the engine to the rider. For some people, all that shaking was too much of a good thing.

Part of the problem was that Harley's customer base was aging. While the average buyer of a Softail in the mid-1980s was a hard-core biker in his mid-twenties, the average buyer in the late 1990s was a professional or experienced tradesman in his mid-forties. The hard-core younger guys wanted the hardtail chopper look and were willing to live with vibration and stiff suspension to get it. The older guys (and a lot of the younger guys, too, to be honest) really wanted a little more comfort.

One way to quell engine vibration and get that comfort is to isolate the engine from the frame in rubber mounts. Most car engines are rubber mounted, and some motorcycle engines are as well. Harley first used them on its FLT Tour Glide for 1980. The Tour Glide and the follow-on FLHT and derivatives such as the Road King use a three-point rubber mounting system that isolates the engine, transmission, and swingarm from the rest of the frame and the rider. That system works really well at most engine speeds, keeping vibes down to a muted throb at anything over idle. The Dynas use a two-point rubber mounting system that is

Above: Beating heart of the second-generation Softail line was the Twin Cam 88B engine, which featured twin counterbalancers to smooth out the legendary vibrations of Harley's 45-degree V-twin.

Opposite: For 2000, the Heritage line included the Classic, Springer, and Fat Boy. Shown is a lowered 2001 Fat Boy with laced wheels.

Above: Twin Cam engines bolt solidly to their transmission. Chrome oil lines replace the rubber lines used on Evo Softails.

Above right: On the Twin Cam Softails, one-piece gas tanks replace the old twin saddle tanks. On the new tanks, the left filler cap contains a gas gauge and is not removable.

stiffer, for better handling, but allows more vibes through to the rider.

Given all that experience, it was natural for Harley-Davidson to try rubber-mounting the Softail. After experimenting with the idea and even building at least one prototype, however, that approach was rejected.

Why?

Looks. The Softail had always been about looks, and those rubber mounts forced compromises in the classic Softail styling that Willie G. and Louie N. were unwilling to accept. You see, those rubber mounts that make the FLT and others so much smoother also allow the motor to dance around in the frame. To get that dancing room, the frame has to be spaced away from the engine, resulting in a frame that no longer has the look of being "shrink-wrapped" around the engine. Styling insisted on keeping the look of the solid-mounted engine.

Thus, styling concerns drove Harley's engineers toward a much better and more modern solution to reduce engine vibration on the Softail. That way required a lot more work to design than rubber mounts, and added complexity to the engine, but it's really the ideal solution: balance out the vibration within the engine itself.

Balancing Act

The enemy in the vibration wars is spinning and reciprocating masses such as the crankshaft, flywheels, pistons, and rods. One way to keep the vibes down is to design the engine so that pairs of cylinders work together to cancel out much of the vibration from each other. This is the approach used by BMW, Moto Guzzi, and others on their twins. That wouldn't work for Harley-Davidson because at the start of the P-22 project that resulted in the twin Twin Cam motors, Willie G. and Styling had insisted on keeping the classic 45-degree Harley Big Twin design.

There was another way, fortunately: if you spin other masses in the engine in opposition to the vibratory ones, you can cancel out the vibrations before they resonate out of the engine. These spinning masses are known as counterbalancers, and Harley engineers early on decided to build two of them into the P-22 Beta's lower end. They placed both parallel to the crankshaft, one in the front of the crankcase and one at the rear. They "tuned" them to cancel out 90 percent of the primary vibration, leaving just enough of the familiar pulse to reassure the rider that a Harley heart still beat within the new Softails.

Each counterbalancer weighs 2.5 pounds, and both are spun by a single chain powered directly from a sprocket on the crank. A pair of hydraulic adjusters keep the chain tight, and the whole works was designed so it would be maintenance-free for the life of the engine.

The rest of the engine was pure Twin Cam 88, meaning basically all-new compared to the old Evolution engine. It was stronger, more powerful, more "expandable," and longer lasting than the old Evo to boot. Some even said its massive fins gave it the edge in looks, too. Engine cases were also built with a stout interface for mounting the transmission solidly to their aft end, turning the engine and transmission into a stiff unit that could then be used to augment the frame.

All that's great, but the counterbalancers gave the Twin Cam B its real character. And that character was "smooth." Fire it up, and you hear the familiar Harley lope, but the other sensations are all eerily different. Evo Softails shuddered at idle like storm-tossed seas. Twin Cam Softails are as glass-smooth as a small lake at sunrise. That smoothness brought a secondary benefit

as well: no longer would Softails be known for shaking off parts as they shuddered down the road.

Second-Generation Transmission

Harley's five-speed transmission was a venerable and durable design but in function it, too, was behind the times. Its long lever throw and emphatic "clunk" when booted into gear were more or less normal when it was introduced for 1980, but by the late 1990s it seemed an embarrassing vestige of Harley's AMF past. Clearly, it wouldn't do for the eerily smooth second-generation Softail.

Harley engineers completely reworked the five-speed for the 2000 Softails to

Back-to-basics models such as the Softail Standard are fitted with an engine finished in silver powdercoat.

Upscale models such as the Fat Boy are fitted with a chrome-and-black engine.

The Standard was introduced in 1999 and was continued into the Twin Cam era as the basic, "roll your own" Softail model.

Left: As Harley intended, the owner of this Standard has customized it to his tastes, with flat bars on tall risers.

Below: Twin Cam Softails were given a completely redesigned frame that was much stiffer than the original frame.

eliminate slop and lash and reduce shifting effort by 50 percent. The result was a tranny as slick as the balanced motor. It still gave a muted clunk when dropped into first, but was a delight to shift, and neutral was a snap to find. Its cases were also redesigned to mate solidly with the engine and improve its appearance.

For model year 2000, the upgraded transmission was available only on the Softail line.

Framing a New Masterpiece

The Softail frame was introduced the same year as the Evolution motor and was given a mild update for 1986, when Harley-Davidson fitted the Softail with the five-speed transmission. By the mid-1990s, it needed an upgrade at least as much as the motor. It still looked good, but it wasn't up to that day's standards for stiffness and suspension compliance—let alone the future's. The boys in Powertrain decided the new Softail engine would bolt solidly to its transmission, so Harley's chassis engineers had to revise the frame to get rid of the old seat post that stood between the engine and transmission. That rigid engine-transmission unit helped stiffen the frame, but the

Left: Even with the new engine, the Fat Boy retained its classic good looks.

Opposite: The Standard brought back the basic look of the original Softail.

engineers designed in even more stiffness and reduced the number of individual parts to make it easier to manufacture.

The chassis boys were getting good at their work, too. With each passing generation of bikes, they had gained more experience designing frames for stiffness and economical construction. All this really began on the FLT of 1980, then the FXR of 1982, and on through the Dyna of 1991 and a bunch of improvements to the Dyna and touring frames in the mid-1990s. They put all that to good use in updating the Softail frame.

Using computers and finite-element analysis techniques, Harley engineers redesigned the Softail frame from axle to steering head. The Harley literature claims it's 34 percent stiffer and is built of half the number of parts. The second claim is hard for an outsider to verify, but one ride confirms the first. The new frame gives a tight, poised feel, where the old felt flexy and uncertain.

The frame was also given a wider swingarm to allow the wider rear tires that had become fashionable, and the rear suspension was heavily revised to give a more compliant ride. For the convenience of everyone and to make it easier to sell in European markets that require an integral fork lock, Harley engineers built one into the steering head of the Softail frame. You can leave your padlock at home now. And it operates off the same key that unlocks the ignition, so you don't even need to carry a second key.

New Gas Tanks

First-generation Softails were fitted with the classic Harley saddle gas tanks, one on each side of the frame backbone tube, which were largely unchanged from those fitted to the Knuckleheads, Panheads, and Shovelheads of decades past. For the second-generation Softail, the company made the switch to an all-new single gas tank that looked like the old dual tanks, as previously

Twin Cam Fat Boys were fitted with the same over-under shotgun exhaust fitted to the Deuce.

Harley-Davidson celebrated its 100th anniversary in 2003 with special paint schemes and detailing on all its models. Shown is a Heritage Classic.

they had on the Dyna Wide Glide and Road King models.

Why go to one tank instead of the traditional twin saddle tanks? It would be easy to say "ease of production" or "cheaper," but I suspect the real reason was a dual concern for the safety of new customers unfamiliar with the quirks of the dual-tank system and Harley's own understandable

need to protect itself from potential product liability suits.

Those saddle tanks looked great and had been part of the Big Twin style since the original Knucklehead of 1936, but they had one big fault: the two tanks are separate vessels, each with its own filler cap, but they are also connected by a balance tube. Say you park your Softail Custom on

Anniversary detailing on the dash of a 2003 Heritage Classic.

its sidestand, pull off the right filler cap and top it off. As you're topping off, you notice the level keeps slowly going down, so you keep topping off until it's full and stays there. Then, you twist off the left cap (you only do this once), and fuel comes gushing out, and keeps gushing until you get the cap back on and sealed or lift the bike upright.

If the engine's hot, you get clouds of gas fumes; if there's a spark source, you get a blowtorch. Not good for bike, rider, or corporate peace of mind. No worries of that on the second-generation Softails. The left cap's a fake, there only to carry forward the style of the dual tanks and to hold the gas gauge.

All of the regular Softail models for model year 2000 wore a 5-gallon single tank—a compromise in width between the old 4.2-gallon (used on all but the Softail Custom) and 5.2-gallon dual tanks. The Deuce was given a unique stretched tank, and we'll get to that soon.

Other Updates

Sealed wheel bearings replaced the tapered bearings previously used. The new bearings needed neither greasing nor adjustment for their projected 100,000-mile service life. A new sealed battery was also maintenance-free.

That cover hides the two camshafts that give the motor its name. For 2003, the cover proudly proclaims "100 Years."

Brakes on the entire Harley-Davidson line had long been at least one generation behind industry standards. Brakes on the Softails were especially poor because they had only a single disc up front. For model year 2000, Harley upgraded the discs on all models with new uniform-expanding rotors and four-piston calipers (the new calipers were used only on the rear of the Springer models). Softails also got an improved rear master cylinder. Even though the Softails still had only a single disc up front, the new discs and calipers gave vastly improved braking and feel.

The Fat Boy's exhaust was restyled to cluster the twin mufflers much closer together, for even more of the over-under shotgun look. Saddlebags on the Heritage Classic were made larger for 2000 and were fitted with quick-release buckles.

To give the Softails more of the old Knucklehead look, Harley engineers rerouted the oil lines between the engine and oil tank to put them right out front. And, as in the old days, they were chromed steel instead of rubber.

Rave Reviews

All those details combined to make the Twin Cam Softails feel brand-new. They still looked like their predecessors, but functionally they were as different as a Dyna Wide Glide is from the original Shovel-powered Wide Glide. First of all, the counterbalancers worked as advertised. They didn't shake the rider or throw parts onto the road. They tracked through turns like a modern bike. The hardtail-look rear suspension actually soaked up the bumps without hammering your back. The brakes scrubbed off speed in modern fashion. In short, Harley's revamped Softail line was ready to carry classic Harley styling into the new millennium.

The stylish oval air-cleaner cover celebrates "100 years of great motorcycles."

The Deuce

Back to the new kid on the Y2K block—a radical new styling statement that Harley-Davidson called the Deuce, representing the second generation of the Softail Custom. It was also tagged with the rather unfortunate "STD" alpha designation. (Perhaps they should have used rubber after all?) Never mind, though, the Deuce set a new standard for cruiser styling because its looks owed more to the best one-off customs of the late 1990s than to the choppers of the 1960s and 1970s.

At the front, Willie G. and Louie Netz fitted new forks, chromed from the axle nut to the triple-trees. Sculpted sliders look like they've been turned from billet. A laced 21-inch wheel with chrome rim and skinny tire carries over the chopper look from the Softail Custom, as does the bikini front fender—but Willie G. and Louie N. gave it a clean, modern look by hiding the mounts behind the fork sliders. High chrome risers carry the line of the forks back toward the instrument console. They're topped by low-rise bars that fall readily to hand, with a

sleek new bullet-shaped reflector-optic turn signal at each side.

Its most prominent new piece is a stretched gas tank that makes the whole machine look longer, lower, and more like a modern machine than a chopped antique. Like the other 2000 Softail tanks, the Deuce's tank is a one-piece design with a filler cap on the right side and a fake cap with real gas gauge on the left. Stretched it may be, but the Deuce tank actually holds a tenth of a gallon less than the regular Softail tank. It's rated at 4.9 gallons. Unique tank graphics and pinstriping and/or two-tone paneling accent the tank stretch.

The chrome-plated crown atop that tank is a unique console integrating the speedometer, indicator lights, and ignition switch into a package that is completely modern in style, yet evocative of the consoles of old.

The black-and-chrome Twin Cam B motor amidships breathes through the same stylish oval air cleaner as the rest of the Twin Cams, but it exhales through a completely restyled over-under shotgun exhaust that it shares only with the Fat Boy.

The seat is deeply stepped for a seat height of only 26 inches, its rider's perch tilted jauntily back to continue the line of the tank-top console. Combined with the forward-mounted pegs, this seat stretches the rider out, too, in classic Softail fashion. Some riders love the position; others hate it. Most find it tolerable for short rides, at least.

Willie and Louie made the Deuce's aft end as distinctive and clean and cutting-edge as its front. The ruler-straight lower line of the new rear fender stretches back to cut the top curve of the fender. A recessed taillight keeps the look as streamlined as a bullet train.

Under that fender is an all-new deep-dish aluminum-disc rear wheel. Styled like the front fan of a jet engine, this disc is

larger and wider than that used on the Softail Custom or Wide Glide. It carries a fat low-profile 160/70-17 tire. That fat new rubber contributed to the Deuce's excellent (for a Softail) ground clearance and rear braking capabilities.

Willie and Louie's attention to detail shows everywhere. Chromed oil lines wind sinuously from the chromed oil tank to the engine and back. The repositioned kickstand is easier to reach from the saddle. Chrome-plated fender supports were redesigned to hide all fasteners. Turn signals are smaller and streamlined to a bullet shape at the rear. Even the tranny cover is chromed.

When the Deuce was introduced to the press on August 1, 1999, it caused almost as big a stir as the original Softail had in 1984. And, like that original Softail's, the Deuce's styling was novel enough to overshadow the new engine that powered it.

The engine got its due on the first test rides, however, and everyone was amazed with how well the counterbalancers quelled vibration. They were equally amazed at the new chassis, commenting that it had more ground clearance than the most sporting Dynas and was one cruiser that was actually a hoot on twisty roads.

Harley's new style leader was also ready to crush the competition in the new century that was about to dawn.

Year 2001 and Beyond

For 2001, all the Softails were offered with the option of electronic fuel injection and a factory-installed security system. Little was changed for 2002 and 2003, except that all 2003 models were dressed up to celebrate Harley-Davidson's 100th anniversary.

What lies ahead for Harley-Davidson and its Softails? No one outside the company really knows, but Harley will probably keep building the counterbalanced Softails as long as the company can get the engines to pass emissions testing. Unfortunately, that may not be all that long, if some of the recently proposed California standards are enacted.

As for the balancers? They've been such a success that Harley-Davidson must be considering a redesign of its touring and sporting Big Twins to get rid of their rubber mounts in favor of a balanced engine. I think it's safe to say that counterbalancers are here to stay, and they're the only piece of the current Softails likely to see service in Harley's third century.

INDEX

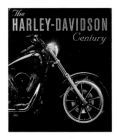
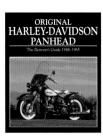

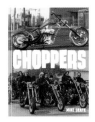